Unusual
Prophecies
Being Fulfilled

UNDERSTANDING *the* PROPHETIC TIMES *and* SEASONS WE ARE IN

UNUSUAL PROPHECIES BEING FULFILLED

JERUSALEM'S MYSTERIOUS CONNECTION *to the* ANCIENT GARDEN *of* EDEN *and* HOW CHRIST WILL RESTORE PARADISE *on* EARTH!

PERRY STONE

UNUSUAL PROPHECIES BEING FULFILLED

Published by Voice of Evangelism Ministries

P. O. Box 3595

Cleveland, Tennessee 37320

Unless otherwise noted, all Scripture quotations are from the King James Version of the Bible.

ISBN 0-9785920-6-9

Printed in the United States of America

This book is the fifth in a series written by Perry Stone under the title, *Unusual Prophecies Being Fulfilled*. Other books are:

Book 1: Unusual Prophecies: Tsunamis, Volcanoes, and Earthquakes in Prophecy

Book 2: Unusual Prophecies: Islamic Prophecies and Terrorism Against America

Book 3: Unusual Prophecies: America's Amazing Prophetic Cycles and Patterns

Book 4: Unusual Prophecies: The Pope, the Eagle, and the Iron Sickle

The International Offices of the Voice of Evangelism

P. O. Box 3595

Cleveland, Tennessee 37320

(423) 478-3456

www.voe.org

Contents

Introduction

What if I were to suggest to you that the ancient Jewish Temples that once were situated on the Temple Mount in Jerusalem were in the same location where the tree of life once stood in the original Garden of Eden?

What if I were to suggest that the rock where the Ark of the Covenant once sat in Solomon's Temple is the same location where God once entered the garden in the cool of the day to commune with Adam (Genesis 3:8)? Could it be that Solomon's Temple was built over the very location where Adam and Eve were created, and only several hundred yards from the fig trees where Adam and Eve hid themselves after eating from the tree of the knowledge of good and evil (Genesis 3:7)?

This might sound like the fabrication of a vivid imagination; but I believe the information in this book will open your spiritual understanding to the astonishing link between the Garden of Eden and the City of Jerusalem in Israel. It will answer questions such as:

- Why did God choose Jerusalem to place His Name and call it His city?

- Why did Solomon place an Eastern Gate just opposite the Mount of Olives?

- Why did the cherub on the Temple veil face toward the east?

- Why was it necessary for Jesus to be crucified and raised from the dead in Jerusalem?

- Why will Jerusalem be the future home of the resurrected saints of God?

For several years I have researched the connection between the Garden of Eden and Mount Moriah in Jerusalem. I have gathered information from many sources and have gleaned from the research of my friend, Robert Vander Maten, as well as Dr. Peter Michas, who years ago began a journey to discover this link. The unveiling of this connection will help you comprehend why Jerusalem has been an embattled city from the very beginning. It will also reveal why Armageddon, the mother of all battles, will be fought to determine who controls Jerusalem.

I believe you will find this to be an intriguing and informative book. I have taught this information for many years during our Holy Land tours. Now you can read the detailed information in the fifth book of the series, *Unusual Prophecies Being Fulfilled*.

CHAPTER 1

Jerusalem: The Earth's Mystical and Mysterious City

It was the trip of a lifetime and an experience that every true Christian dreams about—to see and worship in the holiest city on earth, Jerusalem. On this particular day, our group of one hundred twenty people exited three tour buses on a paved road behind a group of old buildings nestled near the top of the famous Mount of Olives. Most had only dreamt of one day standing where they were, and their excitement was rising like a thermometer on a warm day. About a hundred feet from the group was a large open view of the old city. Turning the corner, we caught our first view of the eastern wall of Old Jerusalem—a view known for two famous markers: the Eastern Gate and the Islamic mosque called the Dome of the Rock, which towers over the center of the historic Temple Mountain.

Without being led, these pilgrims to the Holy Land began waving palm branches as they sang the song, "We Are Marching to Zion". As they turned the corner, I observed the reaction that I have since witnessed many times during our tours to Jerusalem. The singing slowly faded as it was replaced with sniffles and tears. Even those from churches that were not given to spiritual expression were overcome with joy and the reality of knowing that they were now standing on the most sacred piece of real estate on earth. This is the city of Abraham, Melchizedek, David, Solomon, and the Biblical prophets.

Below us in the distance, in a garden called Gethsemane, the very soil had once been saturated by the redemptive blood of Jesus Christ. Deep inside our spirits, we had a sense of knowing that there is something more to this than simply an emotional realization that we are standing on the very land where Jesus and the prophets, patriarchs, and disciples walked.

My Personal Experience

Many years later I stood at the Hebrew University promenade and stared for my twenty-fifth time at the ancient, weather-worn limestone ashlars on the Eastern Wall. My mind journeyed back to the year 1991. That was the year I became obsessed with questions such as: *Why here? Of all the places on the planet, why did God choose this place? Why is this mountain called the mountain of the Lord? What did God know about this place that we do not know today?*

Back in Abraham's day, the Temple Mount was a pearly white limestone hill surrounded by five other mountains. This hill, known in Scripture as Moriah, is 2,500 feet above sea level and certainly was not more special that any other mountain in the sight of God. Or was it? Those questions prompted me to search for the answers, just to satisfy my own curiosity. My research resulted in a conclusion that transformed my personal view of Jerusalem.

One evening in 1991, I was pouring over notes and Scriptures in my room in the Hyatt Regency in Jerusalem. My travel coordinator, Robert Vander Maten, and I were discussing the mystery that shrouded Jerusalem. I had researched information about the possible link between Jerusalem and the ancient Garden of Eden. Robert pulled out a piece of paper and began to sketch the boundaries of the rivers of the garden mentioned in the second chapter of Genesis. I was amazed when he showed me how the boundaries of the ancient Garden of Eden may have been fifteen hundred miles square, and how that Jerusalem was in the center of God's huge garden! Robert began to link my information with the research of Professor Peter Michas, a Greek minister and researcher who had spent much time digging out unique insights that linked Jerusalem to God's first earthly garden.

From that moment on, Jerusalem took on another dimension. The veil that hid the divine mystery surrounding the question "Why did God choose Jerusalem?" began to lift. I now believe that Jerusalem was special because of its link to the first man Adam and the ancient Garden of Eden.

What Does History Tell Us?

When I talk about the Eden connection to Jerusalem, one of the first questions that knowledgeable Bible students ask is, "But wasn't the Garden of Eden located in Iraq or somewhere near the Euphrates River?" This belief is commonly held, since one of the river boundaries mentioned in Genesis chapter two is the Euphrates River, which flows today between Iran and Iraq. The assumption is that, since the Euphrates River was a river in Eden, the garden must have been situated in that area. Those who live in southern Iraq often point to an area they believe was the garden. One archeologist, David Rohl, claimed to have located the site in a lush valley beneath an extinct volcano in Iran. Another archeologist, Juris Zarins, claims that the garden was located where the Tigris and Euphrates Rivers meet in southern Iraq.

Informed Bible scholars, however, debate the original location of the Garden of Eden. *Barnes Notes* states, "In endeavoring to determine the situation (location) of Eden, it is evident we can proceed on probable grounds." In his commentary, Adam Clark commented on the location of Eden by writing:

"It would astonish an ordinary reader, who should be obliged to consult different commentators and critics on the situation of the terrestrial Paradise, to see the vast variety of opinions by which they are divided. Some place it in the third heaven, others in the fourth; some within the orbit of the moon, others in the moon itself; some in the middle regions of the air, or beyond the earth's attraction; some on the earth, others under the earth, and others within the earth; some have fixed it at the north pole, others at the south, some in Tartary, some in China, some on the borders of the Ganges, some in the island of Ceylon; some in Armenia, others in Africa, under the equator; some in Mesopotamia, others in Syria, Persia, Arabia, Babylon, Assyria, and in Palestine. Some have condescended to place it in Europe, and others have contended it either exists not, or is invisible, or is merely of a spiritual nature, and that the whole account is to be spiritually understood! That there was such a place once there is no reason to doubt; the description given by Moses is too particular and circumstantial to be capable of being understood in any spiritual or allegorical way."

–Adam Clark's Commentary

There are almost as many opinions as to the location of the Garden of Eden as there are differences between church denominations. If there are five traditional locations for the garden, then obviously all of them cannot be correct. Because of the lack of archeological or written evidence, tradition dominates the opinions of scholars, thus marking the site in or around the Euphrates River, in the region of Iraq.

Testing the Traditions—The Real Mount Sinai

Traditions can be useful tools, but they are not always accurate. Take for example Mount Sinai, the mountain where Moses received the Ten Commandments (Exodus 31:18). For centuries, Christian tradition placed Mount Sinai in the Negev Desert, between the land of Israel and Egypt. Since the 1800s, tourists have hiked to the top to visit an old monastery where the story of Moses and the Ten Commandments was read and reviewed. Yet the Bible plainly reveals where the real Mount Sinai is located:

> *"For this Agar is Mount Sinai in Arabia, and answereth to Jerusalem which now is, and is in bondage with her children."*
>
> —GALATIANS 4:25

The New Testament indicates that Mount Sinai is in Arabia and not in the Negev Desert. This fact was confirmed several years ago when an American couple, Jim and Penney Caldwell, spent years in Saudi Arabia where they successfully researched and identified Mount Sinai. During their fourteen visits to the mountain, the Caldwell's photographic and video documentation revealed how a granite mountain named Jabal Al Lawz was charred black on the top where perhaps the fire of the Lord came down (Exodus 19:18). They discovered pillars which may have formed the boundaries of the twelve tribes (Exodus 19:12). They also photographed a huge rock that was split, and they captured on tape the evidence of a dried river bed where water had once flowed between the huge rock on what Moses called Mount Horeb, another name for the

Sinai Mountain (Exodus 17:6). On the rocks they found ancient etchings of cows, which may be a pictorial reference to the golden calf worship the Hebrews engaged in while Moses was on the mountain receiving the Commandments (Exodus 32:4-8). Jim also found a fifteen- foot high cave recessed into the mountain, which may have been the same cave used by Elijah when he visited Mount Horeb in First Kings. This photographic evidence was documented in a video called *Mountain of Fire.*

While some scholars reject this evidence since it was not discovered by professional academia, the evidence is convincing. As one Hebrew tour guide said, "The reason Christian tradition places Mount Sinai in the Negev Desert is because it was easy for tourists to reach and more convenient to visit. People can't visit the Arabian area because it is close to a Saudi underground military facility."

Using Mount Sinai as an example, tradition may teach that the Garden of Eden was located somewhere in Iraq between the Euphrates and Tigris Rivers. However, a careful examination of the book of Genesis and the four rivers of Eden gives more details about the boundaries and location of the historic garden. The significance of Eden's location is very important when considering its link to Jerusalem.

CHAPTER 2

The Garden and the Mountain of God

"Thus saith the LORD; I am returned unto Zion, and will dwell in the midst of Jerusalem: and Jerusalem shall be called a city of truth; and the mountain of the LORD of hosts the holy mountain."

—ZECHARIAH 8:3

God's Garden

The Holy Bible begins with the account of creation, a narrative recorded by Moses during his forty years in the wilderness. The first book, Genesis, begins with God creating the heavens and the earth, and climaxes on the sixth day with the Almighty creating Adam and placing him in a beautiful paradise, identified as the Garden of Eden, to care for the garden.

"And the LORD God planted a garden eastward in Eden, and there he put the man whom he had formed." —GENESIS 2:8

Two words should be noted in this passage. The first is the word garden. The Hebrew word garden in the Biblical text is *gan*. This word comes from the Hebrew word *ganan,* meaning "to hedge in or to protect." This word is used eight times in the Old Testament to allude to the protection and guardianship of God. In several of those passages, the text deals with the city of Jerusalem (for example, Isaiah 31:5; Zechariah 9:15 and 12:8). The word, as used in Genesis, implies that God placed man in a secure and happy environment.

Some rabbis believe that the name Eden denotes the larger territory which contains the garden, rather than the name of the garden itself. The Jewish Talmud states that the garden is distinct from Eden (Talmud, Brachos 34b). The Hebrew word *Eden* originates from a word that means "pleasure or delight." The Septuagint translation (the Old Testament translated to Greek) renders this passage, "God planted a paradise in Eden."

The original garden contained every type of tree that produced food and was pleasant to the eyes, including the tree of life and the tree of knowledge of good and evil (Genesis 2:9). These two trees were more than simply fruit trees. Both had a supernatural effect on Adam. The tree of life renewed his entire being and extended his life. Conversely, the tree of knowledge caused Adam's eyes to be opened to right and wrong, and caused guilt and shame when its fruit was eaten (Genesis 3:7).

God's relationship to man in the garden was so special to Him that He entered Eden daily, walking in the cool of the day to fellowship with Adam and Eve (Genesis 3:8). The word cool is the Hebrew word *ruwach* and can allude to the wind, breath, or spirit. The Holy Spirit is called the Ruwach Ha Kodesh. It appears that God either rode a literal wind into the garden, or entered by the wind of His Holy Spirit. David wrote these words:

"And he (God) rode upon a cherub, and did fly; yea, he did fly upon the wings of the wind." — PSALM 18:10

In this perfect setting, a creature more subtle than any others of all creation entered the picture. The serpent suddenly interrupted the serenity of this earthly paradise to introduce a challenge to Eve. He challenged her to eat of the tree of knowledge and be filled with the understanding of the gods (Genesis 3:5). Skeptics often say this account could not have literally happened because serpents cannot communicate with humans. The Jewish historian Josephus commented on this:

> "But while all the living creatures had one language, at that time the serpent, which then lived together with Adam and Eve, showed an envious disposition at his supposal of their living together…he persuaded the woman out of a malicious intention to taste of the tree of knowledge…" — JOSEPHUS BOOK I, CHAPTER I, SECTION 4

This creature communicated in some form to Eve and she fell into the snare of sin. According to the New Testament, the serpent beguiled Eve (2 Corinthians 11:3). This serpent is depicted as Satan, the chief fallen angel of creation. Four times in the book of Revelation, Satan is identified as a serpent (Revelation 12:9, 14, 15; 20:2). At the time God created Adam, sin was already in the universe and Lucifer (Satan) had already been expelled from heaven (Luke 10:18). Satan did not enter the garden as a fallen angel. He did, however, use the serpent as a tool in the same manner that he uses people today to speak for him. One such reference is found in Ezekiel. The prophet addressed the king of Tyre who ruled from Lebanon in Ezekiel's time. In the midst of the prophecy to this king, the prophet traveled back in time to the heavenly paradise of God and wrote about an anointed cherub who was created as a worship leader:

"You were in Eden, the garden of God; every precious stone was your covering: the sardius, topaz, and diamond, beryl, onyx, and jasper, sapphire, turquoise, and emerald with gold. The workmanship of your timbrels and pipes was prepared for you on the day you were created. You were the anointed cherub who covers: I established you; you were on the holy mountain of God; you walked back and forth in the midst of fiery stones. You were perfect in your ways from the day you were created, till iniquity was found in you."

— EZEKIEL 28:13-15 (NKJV)

Most scholars believe this was a picture of Satan, the anointed cherub, before he was cast out of heaven. Ezekiel described a cherub wearing a breastplate with nine precious stones, similar to the twelve-jeweled breastplate of the Old Testament Jewish High Priest (Exodus 39:9-14). In the text, the phrase "timbrels and pipes" reveals that this cherub was created with the ability to make musical notes and sounds. Ezekiel said that he was on the mountain of God. This mountain was the heavenly Mount Zion (Revelation 14:1) where God is presently and continually worshipped by the heavenly angels (Hebrews 12:22).

The phrase, "you were in Eden," can have a double reference to both the heavenly Eden called paradise in 2 Corinthians 12:4 and to the earthly Eden where Adam and Eve originally dwelt. Satan was once in both areas—in heaven as an angel and on earth through a serpent. We know that when the Bible speaks of the mountain of God that it can refer to the sacred mountain in heaven where God's Throne rests, or to the earthly mountain in Jerusalem where both Jewish Temples once existed.

Mountains in Jerusalem

In Jerusalem, there are three mountains that connect to one another:

Mount Ophel, Mount Zion, and Mount Moriah. Mount Ophel is mentioned five times in the Old Testament. Ophel was the southern slope of what is today known as the City of David. The old walls of Ophel connected Mount Zion with the ancient Temple Mountain. Mount Zion was the higher part of the southern region. It was upon Mount Zion where David built the Tabernacle of David and initiated continual worship before the Ark of the Covenant (1 Chronicles 15:1). The extreme northern end and the highest part of these hills was Mount Moriah. The hill of Moriah was where Abraham offered Isaac and Solomon built the first Temple (Genesis 22:2 and 2 Chronicles 3:1). These mountains were called the land of Moriah by God Himself in Genesis 22:2.

The name Moriah is a mysterious name; however, there is a plant that grows on the mountains in Jerusalem that has a shape similar to the Jewish menorah (candlestick). When this plant is crushed, it releases a fragrance. It is called the Moriah plant, a name which some believe forms the original name of the Mount Moriah. This mountain was and is today considered by the religious Jews and Christians to be the true earthly Mountain of God.

"And many people shall go and say, Come ye, and let us go up to the mountain of the LORD, to the house of the God of Jacob; and he will teach us of his ways, and we will walk in his paths; for out of Zion shall go forth the law, and the word of the LORD from Jerusalem."

—ISAIAH 2:3

Since the Almighty's throne room is on a mountain in heaven, and since the earthly Temple of Solomon and the Temple from Christ's time were built on the Mount called Moriah, we can reason that Satan would have been present on both mountains. First he manifested as the anointed cherub who directed praise and worship on the holy mountain in the heavenly paradise. After his fall from heaven, between Genesis 1:1 and

1:2, Satan later manifested as the chief fallen angel who entered God's Garden of Eden, on the earthly mountain of God where the tree of life and the tree of knowledge of good and evil were planted. Through pride, Satan slid from his position of exaltation to that of a slithering snake. The rebellion against God in heaven and the induction of rebellion against God in the garden both occurred on a sacred mountain—both called the mountain of God. In Scripture, the holiest mountain on earth is the mountain where Zion and Moriah meet, thus forming the hill of God.

More evidence can be collected to connect Eden to Jerusalem as we continue to examine the Genesis account.

Eden—in the East

The earth is 25,000 miles in circumference, yet Scripture tells us that there are four corners of the earth: north, south, east, and west. The Bible mentions that the garden was planted in the East part of Eden:

"And the LORD God planted a garden eastward in Eden…"

—GENESIS 2:8 (KJV)

"And the LORD God planted a garden toward the east, in Eden…"

—GENESIS 2:8 (AMP)

"Now the LORD God had planted a garden in the east, in Eden…"

—GENESIS 2:8 (NIV)

In Scripture, the east refers to the region of the Middle East (Genesis 29:1; Judges 6:3; Isaiah 11:14). The Hebrew word for east in Genesis 2:8 is *qedem*. This word means "to proceed, in front of, before, ancient." According to an Egyptian writing (Romance of Sinuhe) written in 1900 B.C., the word east (qedem) is identified as a land near Canaan. The land of Canaan is identified as the early Biblical name for the land of Israel

(Genesis 11:31). Noah's son Ham raised four sons, one named Canaan (Genesis 10:6). The sons of Canaan later formed several nomadic tribes and settled in much of the area that we know today as the southern part of Israel, including the southern section of the Dead Sea. Scholars believe the five cities of the plain mentioned in Genesis 14:2, which included Sodom and Gomorrah, were built in the southern area of Israel.

> *"And the border of the Canaanites was from Sidon, as thou comest to Gerar, unto Gaza; as thou goest, unto Sodom, and Gomorrah, and Admah, and Zeboiim, even unto Lasha."* – GENESIS 10:19

Before the destruction of Sodom and Gomorrah, the southern end of the Dead Sea was compared to the garden of the Lord (Eden) with its beautiful trees, water, and greenery. This comparison is unique, and we will show how Scripture and historical patterns link the land of Canaan with the Garden of Eden.

> *"And Lot lifted up his eyes, and beheld all the plain of Jordan, that it was well watered everywhere, before the LORD destroyed Sodom and Gomorrah, even as the garden of the LORD, like the land of Egypt, as thou comest unto Zoar."* – GENESIS 13:10

Today it is difficult to imagine this area being well-watered and compared to the Garden of Eden! It is a barren, rugged, and dry region surrounded by jagged, rose-colored mountains called the wilderness of Judea. Archeologists have, however, uncovered evidence of five streams that flowed in the area where Sodom and Gomorrah once existed. This information helps to verify that the location was once a well-watered region.

Another series of fascinating clues to the identity and location of ancient Eden can be discovered when examining the main rivers that once formed the boundaries of the Garden of the Lord.

CHAPTER 3

The Four Rivers of the Lost Garden of Eden

"Now a river went out of Eden to water the garden, and from there it parted and became four riverheads. The name of the first is Pishon; it is the one which skirts the whole land of Havilah, where there is gold. And the gold of that land is good. Bdellium and the onyx stone are there. The name of the second river is Gihon; it is the one which goes around the whole land of Cush. The name of the third river is Hiddekel; it is the one which goes toward the east of Assyria. The fourth river is the Euphrates."

—GENESIS 2:10-14 (NKJV)

As previously pointed out, the garden was located in the east. History validates this claim since the regions of Northern Africa, Israel, Lebanon, Syria, and Iraq are known as the cradle of civilization. Archeologists note that one of the oldest known inhabited areas in the world is the region of Jericho, whose mud brick ruins rest just north of the Dead Sea in Israel. Damascus, Syria is the oldest continuing city on earth, having never been totally destroyed by natural catastrophe or a major war. Iraq can boast that their country was the ancient Babylon and the site where the first major skyscraper, a ziggurat called the Tower of Babel, was constructed (Genesis 11:1-9). These facts tend to undergird the theory that human civilization began in the Middle East.

The Cradle of Civilization

The area of the earth known as the cradle of civilization that is located along the edge of Syria and Iraq is also called the Fertile Crescent. The region has several major rivers and water sources that support life and an ecological system. This is also the same land mass where two of the four rivers of the Garden of Eden were (are) located.

One of these rivers, the Euphrates, is recognized by the same name throughout Biblical and secular history. The headwaters of this river begin in eastern Turkey and flow south for 1,700 miles, eventually emptying into the Persian Gulf. The Euphrates is currently the main water source in Syria and Iraq.

The second river that can easily be identified is the Hiddekel, which is mentioned in Daniel 10:4. Daniel was held captive in Babylon and was sitting by the banks of the Hiddekel River when he experienced a vision of a mighty angel of the Lord. According to scholars, the Hiddekel River is identified today as the Tigris River. The headwaters of this river also begin in Turkey and flow south for about 1,180 miles before emptying into the Persian Gulf. This river is presently the physical boundary between the countries of Iraq and Iran.

The two other rivers mentioned in Genesis chapter two are less known, and there is much speculation as to their identities. According to the historian Josephus, the Gihon mentioned by Moses is actually the same river as the Nile. The Egyptians called it the Gihon and the Greeks named it the Nile. But it appears to be the same river and the third boundary river of Eden.

> "…and the Geon (Gihon) runs through Egypt, and denotes what arises from the east, which the Greeks call Nile."
>
> — JOSEPHUS: ANTIQUITIES, BOOK I, CHAPTER I, PART 3

This agrees with the Bible, which indicated the Gihon compassed the whole land of Cush. The early area of Cush is marked on old maps as the region of Northern Africa, including Ethiopia, Sudan, and Egypt. The earliest scholars believed that the Ethiopians were descendants of Cush, the son of Ham, the son of Noah (Genesis 10:6). There is a reference to this in Amos 9:7, where Cush migrated to the land south of Egypt. The *Jamieson, Fausset, and Brown Commentary* says this:

> "The Cushite inhabitants of Southern Babylonia are said by Sir H. Rawlinson to have been of a cognate race with the primitive colonists of Arabia and the African Ethiopia; and this view of their common origin he proves by the identity of their system of writing, which has the closest affinity with that of Egypt; by their language, which is unquestionably Cushite or Ethiopian; by the traditions of Babylon and Assyria, which point to an early connection between Ethiopia, Southern Arabia, and the cities of the lower Euphrates; and by the name of Nimrod being the eponym of the Chaldean race, while those of the other sons of Cush mark the line of colonization along the southern and eastern shores of the Arabian peninsula, from the Red Sea to the mouth of the Euphrates."
>
> —JAMIESON, FAUSSET, AND BROWN COMMENTARY

Since the Nile River flows from the south going north into Egypt, this could be the river that compasses the land of Cush in Northeastern Africa.

The fourth and final river listed is the most difficult to identify. There are several theories as to the location of this Pishon River. Josephus believed the Pishon was the Ganges River running through India. Moses wrote that his area was in the land of Havilah where there was gold. This serves as a clue to identify the area of the Pishon River. The *Adam Clark Commentary* states:

> "He (Hadrian Reland) thinks the Pison was the Phasis, a river of Colchis, emptying itself into the Euxine Sea where there is a city called Chabala, the pronunciation of which is nearly the same with that of Havilah, or Chawiylaah (OT:2341), according to the Hebrew, the waw (w) being changed in Greek to beta (b). This country was famous for gold, whence the fable of the Golden Fleece, attempted to be carried away from that country by the heroes of Greece."

This would place one of the rivers of Eden to the extreme east of the Tigris River toward the direction of India. If two rivers were at the border of Iran and Iraq and the third ran through Egypt, then why would the fourth—the Ganges River—be as far away as India? Another idea is that the land of Havilah (according to the older maps) is the southwestern region of the Arabian Peninsula. Notice this from the *Jamieson, Fausset, and Brown Commentary*:

> "Bochart places it in the southeastern part of Arabia, not far from the Persian Gulf (cf. Gen 10:7, 29), where a large district of that name is mentioned as divided between two different tribes of Shemites and of Hamites, deriving Havilah from a Hebrew root which signifies sand, its sandy character being probably the origin of its designation."

Many historical sources believe the land of Havilah was located in the region of Saudi Arabia. With the Arabian Peninsula being sandy and dry, what happened to the river that once flowed through this region of Eden?

Author James Sauer released information in *Biblical Archaeology Review* (July / August 1996) in which he wrote of special satellite imagery taken over Saudi Arabia. In a ten thousand square mile area located northwest of Riyad, the satellite picked up a jagged seam of limestone rock that was part of a river channel now hidden by sand dunes. This dried river, named the Kuwait River, once cut across the Arabian Peninsula and proves that the region was once a wet area. Mr. Sauer suggests that this river may be the Pishon River associated with one of the four rivers of Eden.

The Pishon flowed around Havilah where there is gold and precious stones (Genesis 2:10-12). There are several areas in Saudi Arabia where gold and precious stones would have been mined. One such gold mine, Mahd edh Dhahab, was rediscovered in 1932 and has been identified as Solomon's mine (1 Kings 9:26-28). This mine, which was active around 1000 B.C., has a rich quartz-sulfide gold vein that still, to this day, produces five tons of gold each year. The fact that this gold mine is located adjacent to the dried riverbed adds further to the suggestion that this was once the bed for the famed Pishon River of Eden.

Through research, it appears that these four rivers and their location can be identified as:

- The Euphrates in Iraq
- The Hiddekel (Tigris) in Iraq
- The Gihon (Nile) in Egypt
- The Pishon in Arabia

The Main River

One of the unusual clues lies in the *main* river that flowed through the entire Garden of Eden. The Scripture says:

> *"And a river went out of Eden to water the garden; and from thence it was parted, and became into four heads."*
>
> —Genesis 2:10 (KJV)

> *"Now a river went out of Eden to water the garden; and from there it divided and became four (river) heads."*
>
> —Genesis 2:10 (AMP)

Moses wrote that one main river ran through the entire garden and, from this one river, four branches (or headwaters) originated. The distance between the headwater of the Euphrates River, which flows near Iraq, and the Gihon River, which flows through Northern Africa, is over one thousand miles! If we begin at the headwaters in Turkey and move toward the beginning of the Gihon in Sudan, then draw lines to indicate the boundaries of the four rivers of Eden, we see that the original garden within these river boundaries may have been up to 1,500 square miles. (The amazing correlation here is that the Holy City New Jerusalem that will come down from God out of heaven is 1,500 miles square according to Revelation 21:16-17).

Scripture names four rivers, and the headwaters are in four different areas of origin. How could these four rivers come out of one main river? Where is this mysterious main river of Eden? What is the name of it, and where is it located today? How can one river form four different headwaters when the four rivers are so far apart from one another?

The *ArtScroll Tanach Series* sheds light on this:

"Hirsch comments that some criticize the geographical description in this verse because it has been taken to refer to a river which divides into four streams, and no such river has been found...But (ra-ashe-im) does not mean branches, but four separate heads. The river starts as a single stream...it eventually disappears into the ground and springs up again in four different locations as four separate rivers."

This has been the question for centuries: how can one river become four rivers in locations that appear to be spread out? The answer may lie in the above commentary, which states that the main river of Eden actually becomes an underground water source that divides into various headwaters, namely the four rivers mentioned in the Bible.

This is certainly possible, as the inspired Scriptures reveal that the garden was watered from a mist coming up from the ground. In Hebrew, the English word *mist* means a vapor or a fog. The NIV version of the Bible translates the word *mist* as streams. Rabbis point out that the Hebrew word for *mist* (ade) is better rendered streams. The garden was watered from moisture and streams from underground water sources.

If Eden was planted in the Middle East and linked to the land of Canaan, then there should be an underground water source—a hidden river located underneath the land of Israel. If Jerusalem is connected to the Garden of Eden, then this source should flow somewhere in Jerusalem. It would be considered the lost river of Eden.

Jerusalem's Underground Water Source

The premier nation that sits between Iraq's Euphrates and Tigris Rivers, the Egyptian Nile, and the Arabian Pishon is Israel. Research indicates that there appears to be a strange and unidentifiable underground water source located both in Israel and Jerusalem.

In the early 1990s, Robert Vander Maten and I requested an interview with a man whom we were informed had conducted secret excavations in and around Jerusalem. His father was from Morocco and, in the 1940s, he had laid new water pipes near the Rockefeller Museum north of the old city in Jerusalem. On one occasion, he broke through the ground into a chamber that was hollow and filled with huge amounts of underground water. He was uncertain of the source of the water and described the noise as a roaring sound, similar to the propeller on a plane.

In 1991 we met with Rabbi Yehudah Getz, one of Jerusalem's leading Rabbis. We engaged him in our theory that Jerusalem was the location of the ancient Garden of Eden. He was intrigued when we mentioned the underground water. He informed us that there was also a large source of water flowing under the Temple Mount in Jerusalem. He said he believed the source may be an underground spring or artesian well that makes its way to Jerusalem from miles away in one of the Arab villages.

This underground water source was confirmed to us when we arranged for an Arab man who guards one of the churches in Jerusalem to allow us to go underground into one of Jerusalem's old churches late one evening after it was closed to tourists. He led us into a small chamber containing an old cistern (a well cut out of stone) and some large clay pots which were relics from the Roman period. We saw the twin pools, located under the Church of the Sisters of Zion. I observed about two feet of water in the small chambers under the church. The gentleman explained that the water had been pumped out of these chambers on several occasions but returns in a matter of days, even when there is no rain. He said it is due to a spring or a water source located underneath the city.

As I will point out later, there will be water from Jerusalem that will flow into both the Dead Sea and the Mediterranean Sea during Christ's one thousand year reign. My point is this: Could this underground water source be linked to the main river that once flowed through Eden? Is there other evidence of an underground river in Israel?

The Sea of Galilee Link

Could this river branch out into other areas of Israel? Does it begin in Turkey, extend through Israel, and flow toward Egypt? There appears to be a mysterious link to the Sea of Galilee, which is actually a lake located below sea level in the mountains of northern Israel. It is a freshwater lake with water continually pouring in from its main feeding source, the Jordan River. The lake contains many fish and is a popular tourist attraction and vacation spot for Israelis.

One type of fish in the lake is a catfish called the korakinos. This fish has been part of the ecosystem in this lake for centuries, including as far back as the time of Christ. Interestingly, this fish is found in both the Nile River and the Sea of Galilee. Mendal Nun wrote a book, *The Sea of Galilee and Its Fishermen in the New Testament*, in which he quotes from the Jewish historian Josephus and mentions the tradition of this fish:

> "This is an unusual fish, the sole representative of its African family…Josephus Flavius refers to the catfish by its Greek name of korakinos, meaning, water raven; he notes that it is found in the Nile. In his opinion, this fact supports the popular belief that there was an underground connection between the Nile and the lake, and that it emerged from below the ground at the largest spring at Tabga."

The Sea of Galilee and the Dead Sea are both located below sea level in what is called the Syro-African rift. This rift is a fault line that begins near the Sea of Galilee in northern Israel and stretches in a straight line south to the Dead Sea. From the Dead Sea, the rift heads south for about one hundred twenty miles and eventually comes to the Gulf of Aquaba, a resort area linking Israel, Jordan, and Egypt. The Jordan River flows from the springs in the Dan (Golan Heights) and empties into the Sea of Galilee. The river continues south, eventually emptying into the northern section of the Dead Sea.

Recently it was discovered that an area off the western coast near the northern part of the Dead Sea also contains a large underground water source. According to a report from *Globes Magazine*, the Israelis discovered a huge underground lake under the Qumran area of Israel, on the Israeli side of the Dead Sea. Some of the water is being pumped from underground and used to irrigate hundreds of plants and trees that recently have been planted in and around the Dead Sea area.

The Actual Boundaries of Eden

If we look at the headwaters of the four rivers and follow the flow of the rivers of Eden, we can see how the land of Eden was not just a small garden in Adam's back yard.* The beautiful garden would have actually extended from the Nile to the Euphrates River and covered the area known as the Fertile Crescent, a region marked from Iraq, Syria, Lebanon, and extending from Turkey into Israel. This is the area where most scholars believe civilization began, and it correlates perfectly with the Eden theory.

As pointed out by Dr. Peter Michas, the most fascinating aspect of the Eden theory is that the boundaries can be 1,500 miles square and *Jerusalem* becomes the center of the Garden of Eden! This could explain one reason why the mountains of Jerusalem are so special to the Lord. It is where He created the first man and planted the tree of life. It is where the last Adam, Jesus Christ, came into the garden area to redeem fallen mankind.

No wonder Jerusalem is so special to God. But the mystery and intrigue continues.

---

* EDEN WAS THE ENTIRE LAND MASS WITHIN THE BOUNDARIES OF THE RIVER. HOWEVER, THE GARDEN WAS IN THE CENTER OF EDEN WHERE BOTH THE TREE OF LIFE AND THE TREE OF KNOWLEDGE OF GOOD AND EVIL WERE LOCATED.

CHAPTER 4

The Tree of Life – Planted on the Future Site of the Temple

*"And out of the ground made the LORD God to grow every tree that is
pleasant to the sight, and good for food; the tree of life also in the midst
of the garden, and the tree of knowledge of good and evil."*

—GENESIS 2:9

If the mysterious tree of life was planted by the Almighty on the same
mountain where the future Temples would be erected, then we can infer
that the two Jewish Temples, one built by Solomon and the second rebuilt
by the returning Babylonian captives, were actually erected on the spot
where God and Adam met for daily communion. It also becomes clear
why Jerusalem is the "apple of God's eye," and affectionately called the
mountain of God. It was the covenant mountain of Abraham, Isaac, and
the Almighty (Deuteronomy 32:10; Genesis 22:1-2). Let us take a look at
several additional keys that were revealed by Moses, linking Adam and
the garden to the future site of the Jewish Temples.

The tree of life supernaturally enabled Adam and Eve to continue living, both physically and spiritually, as long as they partook of the fruit from the tree. John, in the book of Revelation, wrote about the tree of life in the heavenly Jerusalem:

> *"And he showed me a pure river of water of life, clear as crystal, proceeding from the throne of God and of the Lamb. In the middle of its street, and on either side of the river, was the tree of life, which bore twelve fruits, each tree yielding its fruit every month. The leaves of the tree were for the healing of the nations."*
>
> —REVELATION 22:1-2 (NKJV)

Three facts are important:
1. The tree of life is in the midst (center) of the heavenly paradise (Revelation 2:7)
2. The tree of life bears twelve types of fruit (Revelation 22:2)
3. The leaves of the tree are for the healing of the nations (Revelation 22:2)

Apparently, eating from this tree supernaturally sustained Adam and Eve, and produced perpetual physical renewal and healing as they obediently ate from the tree. This tree was planted in the midst of the garden (Genesis 2:9). The Hebrew word for midst is *tavek* and it means "in the center of."

Another unusual tree was located not far from the tree of life and was identified as the tree of the knowledge of good and evil. The text indicates that both trees were located in the same proximity: *"...the tree of life also in the midst of the garden, and the tree of knowledge of good and evil"* (Genesis 2:9).

Satan used a serpent to deceive Eve and cause her to eat from the forbidden tree of knowledge of good and evil. Eve then seduced her husband Adam and their eyes were opened to good and evil, shame, and guilt. Great condemnation gripped the first couple as they hid from God among the trees in the garden. Adam and Eve plucked green leaves from a nearby fig tree and sewed physical coverings to hide their nakedness:

> *"And the eyes of them both were opened, and they knew that they were naked; and they sewed fig leaves together, and made themselves aprons."* —GENESIS 3:7

There were many trees in the garden, but this verse indicates that there were fig trees located in the same area as the tree of life and the tree of knowledge.

As we follow the narrative, we see where God entered the garden expecting Adam to join him in their intimate meeting place at the tree of life. Instead, Adam was hiding like a frightened animal among the trees in the garden. God called for Adam and initiated a series of questions which led to the couple's removal from the center of the garden. In response to God's questions, the blame game began. Adam blamed his failure on Eve while Eve blamed the serpent. The serpent couldn't blame anyone because he was the root of the deception.

Let the Curses Begin

While in the garden, God pronounced a series of curses and separated man from the comfort of the garden for disobedience:

1. The serpent was cursed to crawl upon its belly and eat dust
   (Genesis 3:14)
2. The woman was cursed with pain in childbearing
   (Genesis 3:16)
3. The ground was cursed to produce thorns and thistles
   (Genesis 3:18)

4. The man was cursed to work with the sweat of his brow (Genesis 3:19)
5. The couple was removed through the east side of the garden (Genesis 3:24)
6. Cherubim with a flaming sword guarded the entrance (Genesis 3:24)
7. Cherubim and a flaming sword protected the tree of life (Genesis 3:24)

"So he drove out the man; and he placed at the east of the garden of Eden Cherubims, and a flaming sword which turned every way, to keep the way of the tree of life." – Genesis 3:24

The well-watered garden with its fruitful trees was now behind them, and a barren desolate land of thorns and thistles lay before them. Since cherubim protected the entrance to the garden, it would be impossible for Adam and Eve to return to the tree of life and eat the fruit, thus causing them to forever live in a sinful condition (Genesis 3:23). The garden's path was sealed from the east and human history was forever changed.

Adam—Living Near the Dead Sea?

Where did Adam live after his departure from the center of the garden? Genesis chapter three tells us that Adam and Eve exited the garden through an eastern entrance. God warned them that the ground would be cursed and produce thorns and thistles, and Adam would sweat to make his bread. If we theorize that Mount Moriah (the Temple Mount in Jerusalem) was the center of the garden, then the following scenario could have occurred.

Adam would have exited Mount Moriah through the eastern entrance (gate) of the garden and walked eastward across the Mount of Olives. From the top of the Mount of Olives, Adam would have immediately begun a descent into the wilderness of Judea, ending up at the area near the Jordan River, not far from the Dead Sea. Mount Moriah is approximately 2,500 feet in elevation, while the Dead Sea is 1,300 feet below sea level, making it the lowest spot on earth. The wilderness of Judea and the area surrounding the Dead Sea is rocky and rugged, with high mountains, cliffs, and hills. Today, underground water is used for farming the Jordan rift which runs from the Sea of Galilee south to the beginning of the Dead Sea. However, it required much effort (toil) to farm this region. God cursed the ground and told Adam he would sweat in order to produce the food for his family. I have been in this area in the month of May when it was 115 degrees or higher. Sweat pours from your body. The wilderness is a perfect description of the land as God cursed it.

One of the small clues to indicate that Adam might have settled in this region is the name of a city listed only once in the Bible. Joshua was bringing Israel across the Jordan River when the feet of the priests carrying the Ark of the Covenant touched the water and the Jordan River opened before them, sending tons of water in two opposite directions. To the south, the waters stood as a heap toward the Dead Sea. To the north, the waters were rolled back to an ancient city called Adam:

"That the waters which came down from above stood and rose up upon an heap very far from the city Adam, that is beside Zaretan: and those that came down toward the sea of the plain, even the salt sea, failed and were cut off: and the people passed over right against Jericho."

—JOSHUA 3:16

Archeologists claim that this mysterious city called Adam that was mentioned only in this passage was located about seventeen miles from Jericho and directly north of the Dead Sea. It was located on the edge of the Jordan River, the primary water source for anyone living in this region. It is logical to conclude that the city was named for Adam, and some Rabbis suggest that Adam once lived in this area. Adam was 130 years old when his son Seth was born, and he died at age 930 (Genesis 5:5). He and Eve lived outside the area of the garden and would have needed a water source and a place to reside for all those years.

The city of Adam was situated to the east of Jerusalem. The importance of living on this side of Eden was revealed in the Jewish book of Jasher. This book is mentioned in Joshua 10:13 (*"Is this not written in the book of Jasher?"*) and again in 2 Samuel 1:18 (*"Behold it is written in the book of Jasher."*) This scroll, written in Hebrew, was discovered in the 1800s and translated into English by a British scholar. Although it is not considered inspired, it is considered sacred history. The book of Jasher contains information that fills in the historical gaps of many stories found in the book of Genesis.

> "And the Lord God drove them that day from the garden of Eden, to till the ground from which they were taken, and they went and dwelt in the east of the garden of Eden; and Adam knew his wife Eve and she bare two sons and three daughters."
>
> —JASHER 10:12

Many archeologists agree that the area of Jericho (an oasis throughout history) is one of the oldest areas for mankind on earth. The city of Adam is seventeen miles away, so Adam and Eve would have left the center of the garden, headed toward the east, and settled in the valley near a main water source where Adam was forced to till the ground in the sweat of his brow.

Adam Near Jerusalem

For centuries, Jewish tradition has taught that Adam lived near Jerusalem after the fall. Some suggest that the first altar was built by Adam in the area where the Temple would one day sit. We know that the first two sons of Adam and Eve were familiar with animal sacrifices (Genesis 4:3-4). God Himself slew two animals to cover the bodies of Adam and Eve (Genesis 3:21). Adam certainly discovered the importance of sacrifices and no doubt taught the process to his sons, Cain and Abel.

Other Clues About Adam

After being banished from the garden, Eve conceived and bore two sons—Cain and Abel. During a harvest cycle, Cain brought grain from the ground and Abel brought a young animal to offer to God. The Lord received Abel's blood sacrifice but rejected Cain's grain offering. In jealousy, Cain killed his brother. The Jewish writing of Jasher says that Cain took a plow blade and struck his brother in the head, then buried him in the ground (Jasher 10:27). Perhaps this is why God placed a mark on Cain's head and told him that his brother's blood was crying up out of the ground (Genesis 4:10 and 4:15).

After Cain was marked, he left the presence of the Lord and settled in the land of Nod:

> *"And Cain went out from the presence of the LORD, and dwelt in the land of Nod, on the east of Eden."* – GENESIS 4:16

Nod is an unknown area, but the Hebrew word Nod carries the meaning of wandering and being in exile. Cain was banished from the very presence of God and he wandered eastward, outside the boundaries of the garden.

If the eastern river boundary was the Hiddikel (Tigris) River, then east of the Tigris would be the present country of Iran. It is interesting that, even today in Iran (ancient Persia), there are religious fanatics who kill innocent people in God's name, just as Cain slew Abel over an offering.

The Threshing Floor of Abel

From the time of Adam and throughout the Old and New Testaments, during the barley and wheat harvests, threshing floors were used to separate the chaff from the grain. Many of the battles in the Old Testament occurred during the time of the barley or wheat harvest (Judges 15; 1 Samuel 6:13-19; 2 Samuel 21:9). Harvesting grain was a process that included sowing, watering, planting, gathering, and threshing. Israel's enemies would sometimes invade the farms and steal precious grain from the threshing floors. Because Cain killed Abel at harvest time, the murder itself possibly occurred on a stone threshing floor.

The name Abel in Hebrew is *Hebel*, which the *Dictionary of the Bible* says means, "a breath or vapor," probably because of the shortness of life. The same dictionary speaks of the number of places where the name Abel is used in Israel, and it says that the name Abel in these references probably means a meadow. However, the name Abel is used in the following instances:

Name	Scripture Reference	Location
Abel Maim	2 Chronicles 16:4	near Mount Hermon
Abel Meholah	1 Kings 4:12	near Beth-shean
Abel Shittem	Numbers 33:49	near the Dead Sea
Abel Keramim	Judges 11:33	near Rabbath

Abel Shittim is located in the lower level of the Jordan Valley, and Abel Meholah was located in the northern part of the Jordan Valley, near the city of Beth-shean. This is not far from the ancient location of the city of Adam. Since Jericho is only a few miles from the ancient area of Adam and Jericho is one of the oldest cities on earth, then early man is definitely linked to this area in Israel. I suggest that Abel could have kept flocks while Cain tilled the ground in this area. Despite the heat and barrenness of this region, it is common to see flocks of sheep and goats roaming the hills. If Adam lived near the city of Adam, and Cain and Abel were involved in tilling the ground and raising sheep, then the first murder in history could have occurred in the area known as the Jordan Valley, near the Judean Wilderness not far from Jericho.

This in itself is interesting. In the days of the Temple in Jerusalem, there was a yearly feast called the Day of Atonement (Yom Kippur). On this day the High Priest offered two identical goats as atonement for sin. One was marked for the Lord and the other for Azzazel. Jewish history reveals that these two goats were selected from goats in Jericho. This could indicate another spiritual parallel, as many believe that Cain and Abel were twins, based on the reading of the text in Genesis 4:1-2:

"And Adam knew Eve his wife; and she conceived and bare Cain, and said, I have gotten a man from the LORD. And she again bare his brother Abel..."

It literally says, "She added to bear his bother." The Adam Clark Commentary states: "From the very face of this account, it appears evident that Cain and Abel were twins."

One righteous man was slain (Abel) while the other, Cain, escaped but carried his sin with him, just as one goat was slain representing the Lord and the second escaped into the wilderness bearing the sins of the nation on it. With the two "identical" atonement goats coming from

Jericho, and the two sons of Adam being twins and living near the city of Adam, the parallels of Eden continue.

The Stone of Abel

One of the strongest allusions to Abel's name is found in 1 Samuel chapter 6. On this occasion, the Holy Ark of the Covenant was seized by the Philistines. God smote these enemies and in fear they returned the Ark to the men of Israel. The sacred golden Ark was carried on an ox cart to a city in the tribe of Judah called Bethshemesh. The oxen stopped on a large stone called the "great stone of Abel."

> *"And the golden mice, according to the number of all the cities of the Philistines belonging to the five lords, both of fenced cities, and of country villages, even unto the great stone of Abel, whereon they set down the ark of the LORD: which stone remaineth unto this day in the field of Joshua, the Beth-shemite."* —1 SAMUEL 6:18

Abel, the name of the second son of Adam and Eve, is used in the Bible only in connection to Abel, the brother of Cain and the son of Adam. No other person in the Old or New Testament bears this name. Often in Scripture, names are placed upon certain locations and cities based upon the early history of that area and the person(s) linked to that area. For example, Mount Moriah is called Jehovah-Jirah, meaning God will provide or God will see to it (Genesis 22:14). Bethlehem is called the house of bread because of the massive barley and wheat fields in that area. In the above text, why would a large stone in a field be named "the great stone of Abel?"

Was it named later, as some suggest, after 50,000 men were struck dead for looking into the Ark? Or was it named in memory of the death of Abel? If the second suggestion is correct, then the names of Abel linked to all of these Biblical locations are all found in Israel and not in any nation outside of the Promised Land. I believe this is because Cain killed Abel within the boundaries of Eden, which would have included the Jordan Valley and the same area of the future tribe of Judah. The area of Bethshemesh was part of this area.

The tribe of Judah would become the tribe of King David and the tribe from which Christ would come. This tribe was the closest to the Temple Mountain with their boundaries including Bethlehem and the edge of the Mount of Olives. As mentioned earlier, if Adam was expelled from Mount Moriah and traveled east, he would have crossed the Mount of Olives and traveled through the future area of the tribe of Judah to reach the Jordan Valley. He would have dwelt in an area that he named after himself, the city of Adam.

Other clues also link the area of the ancient garden to Mount Moriah, Israel, and the region of the Jordan River and Dead Sea. Some have said, "The garden was plush and much of this area is rocky and barren. How could this be the area of the garden?" Remember that after the fall, the land was cursed. Also, after the flood of Noah, the land would have undergone a massive change. Trees and vegetation would have been destroyed and the topography of the region would have changed.

Where is the Tree of Life?

Whatever happened to the tree of life that was being guarded in the center of Eden? We know the tree originated in heaven and we will enjoy its fruit in the New Jerusalem as indicated by the Apostle John:

"In the midst of the street of it, and on either side of the river, was there the tree of life, which bare twelve manner of fruits, and yielded her fruit every month; and the leaves of the tree were for the healing of the nations." —REVELATION 22:2

The Eden story in Genesis chapter 3 concludes with cherubim and a flaming sword turning in every direction to guard the entrance to the tree of life:

> *"So he drove out the man; and he placed at the east of the garden of Eden Cherubims, and a flaming sword which turned every way, to keep the way of the tree of life."* —GENESIS 3:24

If the tree of life were presently on earth, wouldn't angels be required to guard it to keep sinful man from eating from a tree that brought endless life? How long did the cherubim remain and what happened to the mysterious tree of life?

On this point, both the Bible and ancient tradition are silent. We know that within 1,658 years and ten generations (from Adam to Noah) the world became so corrupt and filled with violence that God chose to destroy most of the human race through the flood.

It is clear that the flood of Noah caused cataclysmic changes to the surface of the earth. When a person pieces together the continents from a world map, they clearly fit together like a loose jigsaw puzzle. The continents were once one large land mass, but were separated during a great shaking of the earth. This could have occurred in the time of Noah during the flood. Mountains were brought low, valleys were raised high, and entire continents were altered. Certainly trees were uprooted and splits in the earth's surface would have changed the geography.

But Noah and his sons would have known the original location of the garden based upon the words of their ancestors. After the flood, the sons of Noah—Shem, Ham, and Japeth—left their father and settled in three different locations. According to scholars, this is where they settled:

- The children of Ham settled in present-day Egypt, Northern Africa, Arabia, and parts of Palestine.

- The children of Japeth settled in present-day Russia, Northern Europe, and as far as India.

- The children of Shem settled in the area of the Fertile Crescent, Persian Gulf, and parts of Europe.

The lineage of the coming Messiah would fall through the line of Noah's son Shem.

> *"To Shem also, the younger brother of Japheth and the ancestor of all the children of Eber (including the Hebrews), children were born."*
> —GENESIS 10:21 (AMP)

If we account for ancient Jewish belief, it would be Shem, the great-grandfather of Eber, who would make his way back to the site of the original garden, now a mountain of limestone rock and various trees surrounded by mountains. According to Jewish writings, Shem and Eber would become the link to restoring the sacred site and to preparing, by pattern, the future site of redemption. This link can be revealed through a mysterious priest and king named Melchizedek.

CHAPTER 5

Melchizedek: Return to Eden

"For this Melchisedek, king of Salem, priest of the most high God, who met Abraham returning from the slaughter of the kings, and blessed him; to whom also Abraham gave a tenth part of all; first being by interpretation King of righteousness, and after that also King of Salem, which is King of peace; Without father, without mother, without descent, having neither beginning of days, nor end of life; but made like unto the Son of God; abideth a priest continually."

— HEBREWS 7:1-3

God directed a man named Abram to leave his family in Ur of Chaldee (In Iraq) and move to a land called Canaan. After a battle with five kings, and after rescuing Lot and the people of Sodom from captivity, the people and their goods were carried to the mountains of Moriah where Abraham met a king and priest of the Most High God. There Abraham offered the tenth (tithe) to the man whose title was Melchizedek.

The Mysterious Melchizedek Factor

Perhaps the most mysterious person in the Bible is Melchizedek. His name comes from two Hebrew words *melech*, meaning king and *zadok*, meaning righteousness. Melchizedek, meaning King of Righteousness, was not this man's name, but the title given to him. It is similar to the title we give our President, or the title Caesar that was given to the head of ancient Rome. Both Christian and Jewish traditions refer to Melchizedek. Christians use the passages from Hebrews chapter 7 to say that this mysterious figure was Jesus pre-incarnate:

> *"Without father, without mother, without descent, having neither beginning of days, nor end of life; but made like unto the Son of God; abideth a priest continually."* – HEBREWS 7:3

Jewish Rabbis teach that Melchizedek was actually Shem, the righteous son of Noah. After the flood the three sons of Noah—Shem, Ham, and Japeth—all settled in different regions of the world. The Jewish teaching is that Shem came to the mountains of Moriah and initiated the first true priesthood for God on earth. Historically, he was the first priest, and he initiated ministry over four hundred years before the priesthood of Aaron through Moses.

The Jewish historical writings of Jasher mention Melchizedek:

> "And Adonizedek king of Jerusalem, the same was Shem, went out with his men to meet Abram and his people, with bread and wine, and they remained together in the valley of Melech."
>
> —JASHER 16:11

Jasher mentions several times the name of Shem and his great-grandson

Eber. Shem was the first king and priest, while Eber was the man whom the Hebrews were named after. Abraham was called a Hebrew in Genesis 14:13. The word in Hebrew is *Ibriy*, which means "an Eberite or a descendent of Eber." The Jewish people are descendents of Shem through Eber.

Could Shem the son of Noah have been living in the time of Abraham? Yes, according to Scripture. Noah was 600 years old and Shem was 100 years old when the flood came (compare Genesis 5:32 with 7:11). From Adam to the flood is 1,656 years. When we add up the genealogies in Genesis chapter 11, we learn that Abraham was born 1,948 years after Adam. Shem, at age 102, had a son named Arphaxad who was born after the flood:

- Arphaxad was born 2 years after the flood (Genesis 11:10)
- Arphaxad was 35 and begat Salah
- Salah was 30 and begat Eber
- Eber was 34 and begat Peleg
- Peleg was 30 and begat Reu
- Reu was 32 and begat Serug
- Serug was 30 and begat Nahor
- Nahor was 29 and begat Terah
- Terah was 70 and begat Abraham

The above list totals 292 years. When added to the 1,656, the total becomes 1,948 years from Adam to the birth of Abraham. This means that Shem was about 392 years of age when Abraham was born. Abraham was one hundred when Isaac was born (meaning Shem was 492). Isaac was 40 when he married (Genesis 25:20), and Shem would have been 532 years of age. Isaac was not much past the age of 40 when Jacob and Esau were born. If, as the book of Jasher indicates, Jacob went to live with

Shem for thirty-two years, then we can speculate that Shem must have been around 580 years old when Jacob returned home. Shem died at age 600; therefore, we know that he was living during the time of Abraham, Isaac, and Jacob.

Jewish writings and tradition clearly indicate that Shem, the righteous son of Noah, took the title of "first king and priest to the Most High God," which in Hebrew is Melchizedek. In Abraham's time, temples were built to many idol gods and idolatrous priests ministered in these temples. In Abraham and Isaac's day the Tabernacle of Moses and the Temple of Solomon did not exist and would not exist until hundreds of years later. Yet Abraham, God's covenant man, met Melchizedek in Jerusalem and offered him tithe (the tenth) of the spoil from a war victory (Genesis chapter 14).

Melchizedek is identified as the king of Salem. In Hebrew the word is actually *Shalem*, which is linked to the Hebrew word *shalom*. The word means "peace and peaceful." When one says the name *Jerusalem* in Hebrew (y'rushalem), the word *shalem* is present. How interesting that Shem would have settled in the area of Mount Moriah in Jerusalem. He must have known some mystery about this region of the world and known that it was special to God.

The Sacrifice on Mount Moriah

Abraham was 140 years old and Isaac was about 40 when Abraham was instructed by the Almighty God to bring his covenant son to a specific location in the land of Moriah and offer him on an altar.

> *"Take now thy son, thine only son Isaac, whom thou lovest, and get thee into the land of Moriah; and offer him there for a burnt offering upon one of the mountains which I will tell thee of."* —GENESIS 22:2

Liberal theologians scoff at this command and question its authenticity since it would be paganism to offer a human sacrifice. The act, however, was only a test. God knew that Isaac would be spared death. Abraham's willingness to give up his only son on Mount Moriah was a picture of God giving up His only Son on the same mountain.

Genesis 22:4 tells us that, while traveling three days to the land of Moriah, Abraham lifted up his eyes and saw the place afar off. In the English Bible, this sentence leads us to believe that Abraham looked up and saw the location where he would offer Isaac. However, a careful Hebrew word study reveals more insight than casual reading offers. The Hebrew phrase for "the place" is *ha maqowm* (pronounced maw-kome´). The word can mean "a space, a locality, or a condition." However, some Hebraic teachers indicate that the phrase "the place" is a reference to God Himself. God is in all places and ever present; therefore, He is "the place!" In Hebrew, the phrase "afar off" is *me rachowq* (pronounced raw-khoke). It can allude to both space and time. It can mean to see into the distance, but it can also mean to peer into the future.

This verse could mean that Abraham suddenly stopped and saw something in the future about God. What did Abraham see? Genesis 22:7-8 tells us that, when they arrived on the mountain to prepare the wood and the altar for the offering, Isaac asked his father, "Where is the lamb?" Abraham replied, "God will provide himself a lamb for the burnt offering." Moments later a ram was placed on the altar in Isaac's place. Why wasn't a lamb placed on the altar since this is what Abraham predicted? I believe Abraham was predicting something about the future and not about his present time.

Abraham foresaw a time when God would place His ultimate sacrifice on the mountain where he and Isaac were standing. He saw something about the future—about the mountain. This conclusion must be correct, because after the ram was offered, the next verse in Scripture reads:

> *"And Abraham called the name of that place Jehovah-Jireh; as it is said to this day, In the mount of the LORD it shall be seen."*
>
> —GENESIS 22:14

The Hebrew phrase *Jehovah-Jireh* means "God will see to it." Moses, who wrote the Genesis account, knew that something special would be seen in the Mount of the Lord in Jerusalem. Did the king-priest Melchizedek unlock a future mystery to Abraham when they met in Jerusalem about seventy years earlier (Genesis chapter 14)? Or did Abraham receive a vision of the future when he lifted up his eyes and saw the mountain of Moriah? In the New Testament, Jesus indicates that Abraham saw into the future:

> *"Your father Abraham rejoiced to see my day: and he saw it, and was glad."* —JOHN 8:56

Thousands of years later, the events surrounding the crucifixion of Christ correlate with the offering of Isaac on Mount Moriah. This correlation is so perfect that it indicates that Abraham did receive some form of divine revelation concerning a future event that would transpire on Mount Moriah. He knew there would be a lamb that God would provide as a sacrifice on this mountain. Remember, this was hundreds of years before the Hebrews would build a Temple on the same mountain where Abraham and Isaac offered a ram on the altar.

The similarities between Abraham and Isaac in the Genesis chapter 22 account and the crucifixion of Christ are listed below:

1. Abraham led Isaac to Jerusalem and God led Christ to Jerusalem.

2. Abraham took Isaac to the top of Mount Moriah and Christ was taken to the top of the hill.

3. Abraham saw the place the third day and Christ was raised the third day.

4. Abraham had Isaac carry the wood and Jesus carried a cross made of wood.

5. Isaac was laid on wood and Christ was laid on a cross of wood.

6. There were two other men with Isaac and there were two other men crucified with Christ.

7. Abraham said God would provide a lamb and Jesus was called the Lamb of God.

8. Isaac got up from the altar and Jesus got up from the grave.

The offering of Isaac was acted out in Jerusalem on one of the mountains in the land of Moriah. Abraham called this place "the Mount of the Lord" (Genesis 22:14). Bible scholars identify the location as the present day Temple Mount in Jerusalem where the Temples of Solomon and Herod once sat, and where the Islamic Mosque—the Dome of the Rock—has been erected.

The Mountain of the Lord

The Temple Mount is linked to several traditions. One very early tradition says that when God formed the heavens and the earth, He stood above the Temple Mount when He completed His creative process. Another tradition is linked to the large stone that lies exposed inside the Islamic

Dome of the Rock. This stone is called the foundation stone, and it is also linked to the time of creation. Jewish sages state that the Holy Temple itself was the center of the mountain; that the mountain was the center of Jerusalem; that Jerusalem was the center of Israel; and that Israel is the center of the world. This could be what God meant when Ezekiel wrote the following:

"Thus saith the Lord GOD; This is Jerusalem; I have set it in the midst of the nations and countries that are round about her." – EZEKIEL 5:5

The Mountain and Isaac

The Bible mentions Mount Moriah, the future Temple Mount, twice—first in the narrative with Abraham and Isaac in Genesis 22:2, and then in reference to Solomon's Temple in 2 Chronicles 3:1. The book of Jasher mentions two other references. In chapter twenty-six it mentions that, in the fifty-ninth year of Isaac's life, his wife Rebecca was still barren. Rebecca recounted how that Abraham had prayed for Sarah to conceive, and she requested that Isaac pray for her to conceive. The writer states:

"…And his wife rose up and went to the land of Moriah to pray there and to seek the Lord, and when they had reached the place Isaac stood up and prayed to the Lord on account of his wife because she was barren." – JASHER 26:5

According to this narrative, she then conceived twins and, after about seven months, they began to struggle within her. (The Biblical account can be found in Genesis 25:21-22.) The writer of Jasher alleged that Rebecca wanted to know why the conflict was occurring among her twins:

"And she said unto them, Why am I alone in this amongst all the women that are upon the earth? And she went to the land of Moriah to seek the Lord on account of this; and she went to Shem and Eber his son* to make inquiries of them in this matter, that they should seek the Lord in this thing respecting her."

—JASHER 26:10

It is logical to assume that since Melchizedek was Shem (Noah's first son) and the Jewish nation took the name Hebrew (from Shem's great-grandson Eber), and Melchizedek was king and priest of Salem (Mount Moriah), that the Mount of Moriah was a sacred spot, considered by the Hebrews to be holy and special above all mountains on earth. Apparently, Shem knew something about this mountain that was passed down from the ten generations of men to Noah.

Jacob Trained by Shem and Eber

According to the author of Jasher, when Isaac's son Jacob was a young man, Isaac sent him to Shem and Eber for spiritual instruction:

"And at that time, Isaac sent his younger son Jacob to the house of Shem and Eber, and he learned the instructions of the Lord and Jacob remained in the house of Shem and Eber for thirty-two years, and Esau his brother did not go for he was not willing to go, and he remained in his father's house in the land of Canaan."

—JASHER 28:18

A story from the Bible begins to take on new insight when we understand the important link between Shem and Mount Moriah. Jacob was journeying, running from his brother Esau. While sleeping on the ground, he had a strange vision. He saw a ladder extending from the ground into heaven with angels ascending and descending on it and God at the top. When Jacob awoke, he said:

> *"And Jacob awaked out of his sleep, and he said, Surely the LORD is in this place; and I knew it not." And he was afraid, and said, How dreadful is this place! This is none other but the house of God, and this is the gate of heaven."* —GENESIS 28:16-17

> *"And he called the name of that place Bethel: but the name of that city was called Luz at the first."* —GENESIS 28:19

For years I pondered the location of the place where Jacob's vision occurred. The Bible says he called the name of the place Bethel, which means the House of God. The land where Jacob laid his head was identified as the gate of heaven. I knew that the Temple Mount in Jerusalem was considered the gate of heaven and identified as the House of God when both Solomon and Herod's Temples existed. It was identified as such because the prayers of God's people rested over the golden altar in the Holy Place, and each morning an appointed priest burnt holy incense on the altar as the words from the prayers ascended from the altar into heaven. The burning sacrifices, the incense, and the worship entered the gate of the heavenly Temple from the Temple Mountain in Jerusalem. It was also the place where the High Priest entered the Holy of Holies once a year to make atonement before the Ark of the Covenant.

At the time of Jacob's vision, the Tabernacle of Moses and the Jewish Temples had not been constructed and would not be erected until hundreds of years later. However, the ground where Solomon would build the House of God was already identified by Melchizedek and Abraham and was marked as the mountain of the Lord!

For many years I believed that, when Jacob identified the gate of heaven and the house of God, he was referring to the area of Mount

Moriah. No other location in all of Israel is as sacred as Jerusalem and no mountain is as holy as Mount Moriah.

In the early 1990s, I was discussing the vision of Jacob's ladder with head Rabbi Yehuda Getz in his office near the Western Wall in Jerusalem. I asked him where Jacob had the vision of the ladder that reached from heaven to earth. Rabbi Getz replied, "Jacob was on the Mount of Olives and the ladder was sitting on the Temple Mount, on Mount Moriah."

Personally I had always believed this but knew that, in the Biblical narrative, there was no specific information about this place, other than it was once called Luz. The word *Luz* is a word referring to some type of nut tree—perhaps an almond tree. In Moses' day, the almond was considered a holy fruit. The rod of Aaron was made from the branch of an almond tree (Numbers 17:8).

Once more, if we turn to Jewish sacred history, we read about where Jacob experienced this vision:

> "And Jacob went forth continuing his road to Haran, and he came as far as Mount Moriah, and he tarried there all night near the city of Luz; and the Lord appeared there unto Jacob on that night, and he said unto him, I am the Lord God of Isaac thy father…"
>
> —JASHER 30:1

The fact that Luz is linked to Jerusalem can be discovered by carefully reading this verse in Genesis:

> *"So Jacob came to Luz, which is in the land of Canaan, that is, Bethel, he and all the people that were with him."* —GENESIS 35:6

The name Luz was identified with Bethel, the word in Hebrew for "House of God." This story reveals that while at Luz, Rebecca's nurse died and was buried under an oak tree (Genesis 35:8). God later revealed

Himself again to Jacob, and he built a pillar and called the place Bethel. The following verse is a clue:

"And they journeyed from Bethel; and there was but a little way to come to Ephrath: and Rachel travailed, and she had hard labor."

—GENESIS 35:16

The area of Ephrath is today Bethlehem. In fact, Bethlehem is called Bethlehem Ephrath. Today, near the entrance to modern Bethlehem is the grave of Rebecca, who died while giving birth to Benjamin. The Scripture says that there was a little way from Bethel to Ephrath. From Jerusalem to Bethlehem is only about eight miles, which could be considered a little way. So, we see that Luz was a city near Mount Moriah, later called the House of God by Jacob.

Mount Moriah was marked by Melchizedek, the first king and priest of God to live in Jerusalem. This is why Abraham carried Isaac to the top of Mount Moriah and built a covenant altar, eventually offering the ram in place of Isaac. According to sacred Jewish history, Isaac prayed for Rebecca there; Jacob was educated there; and Jacob identified the gate of heaven as being located there—on the future House of God!

The Jebusites and Jebus

From the time of Jacob's vision until the return of the Hebrews from Egyptian captivity is several hundred years. The next mention of the sacred mountain of God is when Joshua commanded the children of Israel to drive out the inhabitants of the Promised Land and possess their inheritance. One tribe, called the Jebusites, controlled a city called Jebus. According to Joshua 15:63, Jebus was the city of Jerusalem. The word Jebus comes from a Hebrew root word *buwc* (pronounced boos), meaning "to tread under foot." Biblical history, as you will learn, identifies the large rock on Mount Moriah (which is visible inside the Dome of the Rock) with a threshing floor.

The large stone that makes up the entire Mountain of Moriah was used in Biblical times as a major threshing floor to separate grain in the time of harvest. Israel conquered the Promised Land in Joshua's time but co-existed with the Jebusites during and after the time of Joshua.

David Seizes Jebus

From the time of Abraham to David, the main capital of the Promised Land was Hebron, the burial place of Abraham, Isaac, Jacob, Sarah, Rebecca, and Leah (Genesis 23:19). David knew that he must seize the city of Jebus and begin to build the city of David on the hills of Mount Zion. David eventually captured the stronghold and the castle of Zion:

"And David and all Israel went to Jerusalem, which is Jebus; where the Jebusites were, the inhabitants of the land." –1 Chronicles 11:4

After David captured the mountain of Zion, he built the famous city of David on the side of the hill (2 Samuel 5:9). He later prepared a tent to house the Ark of the Covenant. This tent, called the tabernacle of David, was a center of continual worship where music, singing, and prophesying occurred (1 Chronicles chapter 15). The tent also housed the Ark of the Covenant which David brought up to Jerusalem (1 Chronicles chapter 15; 2 Samuel chapter 6).

The holy Mountain of Moriah in David's time was owned by a man named Araunah. Toward the conclusion of David's life, he numbered Israel and forgot to collect the half shekel of redemption (Exodus 30:12-13). This action initiated a sudden judgment of God upon Israel, and an angel of death swept through the nation and slew over seventy thousand men (2 Samuel 24:15). As the angel approached the Mount of Olives with his eyes set on destroying the men in Jerusalem, David made a sudden decision that would change the course of history.

David ran to the top of the sacred hill and asked Araunah if he would sell the mountain, the threshing instruments, and the oxen. Araunah immediately offered to give the king the mountain at no charge, but David refused saying, "I will not take that which cost me nothing" (2 Samuel 24:24). After David purchased the mountain, he built an altar and offered the blood sacrifice. After that, the plague ceased. This mountain would later become the property of King Solomon, who would construct the most magnificent Temple in world history!

The Mountain was Secure

For the first time since Melchizedek, the sacred mountain of the Lord was secure in the hands of a Hebrew king, David. It was David's desire to build a house for the Lord to dwell—a holy Temple for God's glory. However, David was a man of blood and war, and God refused him the privilege to erect a sacred house on the Mountain of Moriah. The Almighty did, however, permit David's son Solomon to receive plans from David for the construction of this costly project (1 Chronicles chapter 28).

David is called a prophet in the Bible, and Solomon is labeled one of the wisest men who ever lived (Acts 2:29-30; 1 Kings 4:30). Just as Moses received a heavenly vision of the details of the Tabernacle in the wilderness, David received what he called the "pattern of the chariot of the cherubim" (1 Chronicles 28:18). David said:

> *"All this, said David, the LORD made me understand in writing by his hand upon me, even all the works of this pattern."*
> — I CHRONICLES 28:19

Moses received a pattern of the heavenly Temple and created the Tabernacle in the wilderness after that pattern. David received a revelation of the pattern for the Temple, and Solomon took the instructions from paper and created a house of stone and gold. This pattern is more than that of an architect designing a building. It was a re-creation of the Garden of Eden—a place where God could come down once again, on Yom Kippur—and stand near a chosen man, a high priest, on the spot where in ages past the tree of life flourished.

---

*JASHER MAY HAVE CALLED EBER THE "SON OF SHEM" BECAUSE OF THE WAY THE GENEALOGIES MENTION THE LINK BETWEEN SHEM AND EBER: "AND UNTO SHEM ALSO, THE FATHER OF ALL THE CHILDREN OF EBER..." IN GENESIS 10:21. YET, AS YOU CONTINUE TO READ, THE BIBLE REVEALS THAT SHEM WAS THE GREAT-GRANDFATHER OF EBER. JASHER MAY ALSO HAVE REFERRED TO HIM AS A SON BECAUSE OF THE SPIRITUAL TRAINING HE RECEIVED FROM SHEM—IN THE SAME MANNER THAT PAUL ADDRESSED TIMOTHY AS HIS SON, EVEN THOUGH THEY WERE NOT NATURALLY RELATED.

Photo 1: Temple Mount
Why did God choose Jerusalem to place His name (Deuteronomy 12:11) and mark the mountain for the Holy Temple? Could the "Holy Mountain" where the dome now sits be the center of the ancient Garden of Eden?

This photo is St. Catherine's Monastery, the Traditional Mt. Sinai

Photo 3: The Moriah Plant
Mount Moriah may have derived its name from this plant, called the Moriah plant, which grows in Jerusalem. It looks similar to a Menorah and gives off a fragrance when crushed.

Photo 2: The Real Mount Sinai
According to evidence collected by Jim and Penny Caldwell, the real Mount Sinai is in Arabia. Documented in the video "Mountain of Fire", this concept is confirmed in Galatians 4:25, which mentions "Mount Sinai in Arabia."

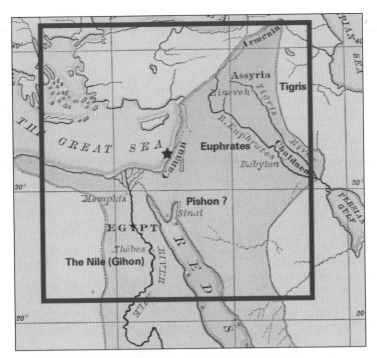

Photo 4: Rivers of Eden

When drawing the boundaries of the four rivers of Eden, the land mass within the borders forms an area of 1,500 square miles. This is the same dimension of the New Jerusalem in Revelation 21:16-17. (Jerusalem location: see star above)

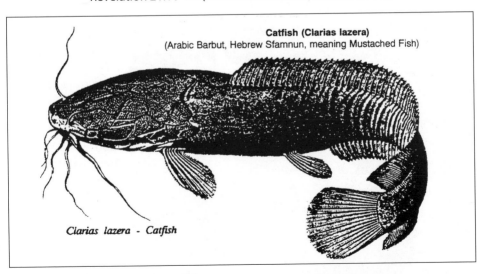

Catfish (Clarias lazera)
(Arabic Barbut, Hebrew Sfamnun, meaning Mustached Fish)

Clarias lazera - Catfish

Photo 5: The Special Catfish

The Korakinos (water raven catfish) is found in the Nile River and the Sea of Galilee, supporting the popular belief that there was an underground connection between the Nile in Egypt and the lake, through the springs that emerge from beneath the ground at Tabga in Tiberias.

Oasis (City) of Jericho

Photo 6: The City of Adam
The city of Adam, today called Tell-Adamiyeh or Damia in Jordan, was located just above Jericho, which is recognized as the oldest city on earth. Adam may have lived in this area after his expulsion from the garden, thus giving the area its original name (Joshua 3:16).

Photo 7: The Ancient Temple
The imagery of the ancient Temple points to the Eden pattern, from the High Priest meeting God at the Ark of the Covenant, to the Cherubim guarding the entrance, to the main entrance being from the east.

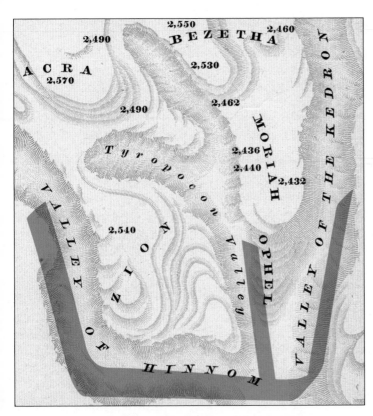

Photo 8: The Letter Shin

God "placed his name" on the mountain of Jerusalem. The mountains and valleys of old Jerusalem form the Hebrew letter *shin*, the 21st letter of the Hebrew alphabet, which represents the name of God. The letter *shin* is also on every mezuzah, the sacred object placed on the door of Jewish homes.

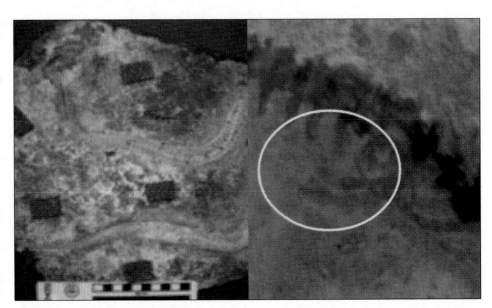

Photo 9: The Serpent with Legs
A fossil found in Ein Yabrud near Ramallah in the Israeli West Bank revealed a serpent with two small hind legs. These were considered the most primitive ever found, revealing that the serpent once walked upright before being cursed to its belly (Genesis 3:14).

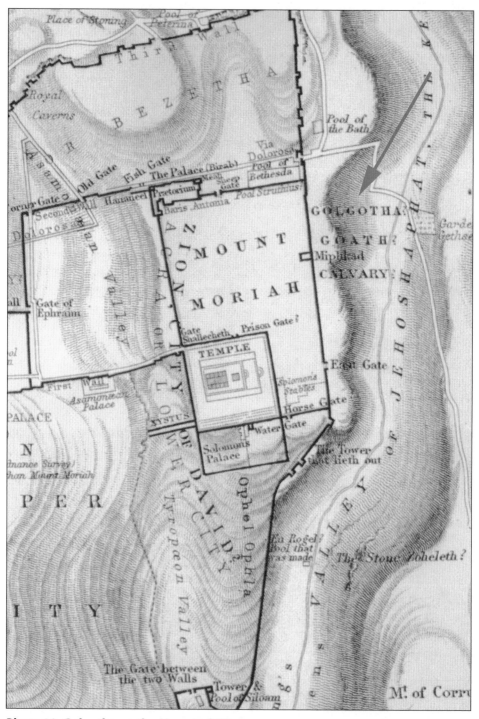

Photo 10: Golgotha on the Mount of Olives

Notice this old Bible map that mentions Golgotha's location outside the Eastern gate near the Mount of Olives. From the Mount of Olives a person could see the veil in the Temple, where the doors were opened.

Photo 11: The Water near the Dead Sea
Huge amounts of underground water are located under the area of Qumran, near the Dead Sea. When Christ returns, the Mount of Olives will be split, releasing this water to pour into the Dead Sea, bringing needed life to the Sea (Ezekiel 47). This could be part of the lost river of Eden.

Photo 12: Jesus' Ministry
Notice that Christ was baptized in the Jordan River and tempted by the devil near Jericho, not far from the location of the city of Adam. Christ was the second man Adam (I Corinthians 15:45), was recognized as God's son and tempted by Satan in the same area where the first Adam had been defeated by the enemy.

City of Adam

Tree of Knowledge

Crucifixion Site

Red Heifer Altar

Tree of Life

Notice the possible locations of the major sites mentioned in this book.

CHAPTER 6

The Eden Pattern and the Temple of Solomon

"Then Solomon began to build the house of the LORD at Jerusalem in Mount Moriah, where the LORD appeared unto David his father, in the place that David had prepared in the threshing floor of Ornan the Jebusite." – 2 CHRONICLES 3:1

God has always used spiritual patterns to reveal His deepest mysteries. In the New Testament, the Greek word for pattern is *tupos*, and it means "a fashion, a figure, a print." A pattern is a picture or a copy of the original. Moses built the tabernacle after the pattern of the heavenly Tabernacle (Hebrews 8:5). There are many patterns in prophecy, in Biblical numbers, and in the imagery of the Tabernacle and the Temple in Jerusalem. When studying how Solomon constructed the House of the Lord on Mount Moriah, it is exciting to see the patterns hidden within which appear to indicate that Solomon had the ancient Garden of Eden in mind when he built the House of the Lord.

Heaven on Earth

The large white limestone rock called Mount Moriah served as the foundation stone (bedrock) inside the Holy of Holies in Solomon's Temple. Just as in Moses' Tabernacle, the Ark of the Covenant was the central piece of sacred furniture. Solomon placed the Ark under the wings of two large cherubim made of olive wood and covered with gold. One wing of each angel touched above the Ark, while the other wing touched the walls behind where they stood (2 Chronicles 3:11-13). These golden angels stood as silent guardians over the Ark, which was a miniature throne of God on earth. When it was transported in Moses' day, four Levites bore the Ark on their shoulders (1 Chronicles 15:15). These four priests were a pattern of the four angels who carry the throne of God as seen in the vision of the prophet Ezekiel (Ezekiel chapter 1).

Directly before the Ark was a large veil with beautiful cherubim embroidered on the curtain (Exodus 26:31). The veil hid the Ark and separated the people from entering the Holy of Holies. The Hebrews saw only the outline of the cherubim and never the inner chamber of the Holy Place.

When Solomon constructed the Temple on the mountain, he also constructed several gates which led into the city and to the Temple of God. The main gate for both Solomon and Herod's Temple was the Eastern Gate, also known as the King's Gate. Little is known about this gate from the time of Solomon. However, this gate was well known in the time of Christ. It was called the Golden Gate, and the "gate called beautiful" (Acts 3:2). It served as the main entrance leading into the Temple from the east side. When a worshipper who traveled from the Judean Wilderness from the east reached the top of the Mount of Olives and looked down on Mount Moriah, they would see the Eastern Gate.

If the gates of the Temple were opened, they could have seen the veil with the cherubim silently and symbolically guarding the entrance to the presence of God.

The massive and expensive Temple of Solomon took seven years to complete. All of Israel gathered on Mount Moriah and countless animals were offered to God as a sacrifice. As the priests began to sing and worship God, the glory of the Lord fell upon the mountain and the priests could not even stand to minister (2 Chronicles 5:14). This Temple would become the meeting place between God and Israel for 480 years.

The Temple Link to the Garden of Eden

Let us examine these three aspects of Solomon's Temple that have a unique link to the Garden of Eden:

1. The rock where the Ark of the Covenant sat;

2. The design of the veil that separated the Holy Place from the Holy of Holies;

3. The Eastern Gate used as the entrance and exit gate of the Temple.

Let us begin with the theory that the tree of life where God originally met with Adam once sat on the Temple Mountain in the same area where the Holy of Holies was once positioned in Solomon's Temple.

First, the Ark of the Covenant in the Temple was placed upon the bedrock of Mount Moriah. Even today, researchers note a rectangular niche cut into the foundation stone inside the Dome of the Rock and identify it as the spot where the lost Ark of the Covenant once rested in the days of the Temple. Once a year on Yom Kippur (the Day of

Atonement), God would come down above the wings of the cherubim on the golden Ark of the Covenant and meet with the High Priest (Exodus 25:22).

This setting in Solomon's time created imagery from the past, during a time when God descended to the garden at the cool of the day to fellowship with one man, Adam. At that time, Adam was sinless and had continual access to the tree of life. At the Temple, however, only on the Day of Atonement did one man, the chosen High Priest, step past the veil into the Holy of Holies. The priest had to be without sin in order to meet with God, who communed from above the wings of the Cherub on the mercy seat of the Ark of the Covenant (Exodus 25:20-22).

The second link is the man-made woven veil that kept all of Israel from gaining access to the resting place of the Ark in the Holy of Holies. Cherubim were sewn into the fabric. The veil forbade common men from entering into the sacred chamber and standing upon the sacred rock or gazing upon the Ark in the Holy of Holies.

This imagery again points back to Eden. This was a pattern of the cherubim with the flaming sword guarding the entrance to the tree of life in the garden. After the fall, Adam was forbidden to enter and was restrained by the guardian angels that overshadowed the entrance with a sword of fire at the garden's entrance.

Let's now look at the Eastern Gate. Both Moses and Solomon, by divine revelation, set up one main entrance on the east, facing the Holy of Holies. In Moses' time, the entrance was a large curtain on the east end of the Tabernacle where the leading tribe of Judah camped. In Solomon's Temple and in the time of Christ, there was one main outer gate facing the east, which was the only way in and out.

The fact that Adam was expelled from Eden from the eastern entrance of the garden is proven by the fact that the cherubim were placed on the east side to prevent the couple from reentering:

> *"So he drove out the man; and he placed at the east of the garden of Eden Cherubims, and a flaming sword which turned every way, to keep the way of the tree of life."* – GENESIS 3:24

In Hebraic thought, the east side is always considered the holy side because the sun rises in the east. The morning services at the Temple could not start until the rays of the sun were seen just above the Hebron Mountains. Thus, the ancient Jewish Temple on Mount Moriah was a visible portrait of God's plan to redeem mankind back to Him and restore the original face–to–face fellowship once experienced in Eden. You may recall that, when Adam and Eve sinned, God Himself slew two animals and covered the first couple's nakedness with the freshly slain skins of the first blood sacrifice:

> *"Unto Adam also and to his wife did the LORD God make coats of skins, and clothed them."* – GENESIS 3:21

This unusual act of God's mercy was performed *before* the couple was physically expelled, meaning it occurred *within* the center of the Garden of Eden. Centuries later, at both Temples on Mount Moriah, a lamb would be offered in the morning and evening. Sin and guilt offerings would be slain and burnt on the outer court's brass altar, in the shadow of the Holy of Holies. Was this act of offering two lambs a visible reenactment of God slaughtering the first two animals to cover the guilt of Adam and Eve?

The early history of Mount Moriah from Genesis chapter 14 (Salem) and Genesis chapter 22 implies that there is a unique connection of God to this area of the world. This special link is also seen in the unusual pattern and shape of the mountain, as it relates to the Hebrew alphabet.

God's Name on the Mountain

The Almighty told Moses that He chose Jerusalem to be the place where He put His name:

> *"But unto the place which the LORD your God shall choose out of all your tribes to put his name there, even unto his habitation shall ye seek, and thither thou shalt come; And thither ye shall bring your burnt offerings, and your sacrifices, and your tithes, and heave offerings of your hand, and your vows, and your freewill offerings, and the firstlings of your herds and of your flocks."* – DEUTERONOMY 12:5-6

Several times in Deuteronomy, Moses mentions a place where the Lord would choose to place His name (12:5; 12:21; 14:23). This could hold several meanings.

The first meaning could be the name Jerusalem. The area was called Luz, then Jebus, then Zion, and eventually Jerusalem. The name Jerusalem comes from two previously mentioned events in Abraham's life. Abraham met Melchizedek in Salem, or Shalem. Years later, when God provided a ram for a sacrifice instead of Isaac, Abraham called the place Jehovah-Jireh. The two words combined, Jirah and Shalem, form the name Jerusalem. The name Jerusalem contains one of the names of God: Jireh, meaning "He will see to it."

A second possible meaning may allude to the shape of the mountains of Ophel, Zion, and Moriah. If the buildings within the old city of Jerusalem were all removed and the typography and shape of the three hills could be seen, the shape of the mountains are similar to the twenty-first letter of the Hebrew alphabet, the letter shin.

The Hebrew letter shin has maintained the same basic form since the beginning of the Hebrew alphabet. Its shape is similar to the English letter W. If you were to look down from the sky onto the Temple Mountain, you would see that the hills and valleys form a shape similar to the Hebrew letter shin. Just below the Mount of Olives is the Kidron Valley. It curves around and meets the valley of Hinnom on the western side of Jerusalem. In between is the Tyropoeon Valley. The formation of these valleys takes a shape similar to the letter shin.

The letter shin is also linked to the blessing of the priest. In Numbers chapter 6 is the famous blessing that Aaron and his sons prayed over the children of Israel:

> *"Speak unto Aaron and unto his sons, saying, On this wise ye shall bless the children of Israel, saying unto them, The LORD bless thee and keep thee: The LORD make his face shine upon thee, and be gracious unto thee: The LORD lift his countenance upon thee, and give thee peace. And they shall put my name upon the children of Israel; and I will bless them."* — NUMBERS 6:23-27

When the High Priest raised both hands and blessed the children of Israel, he formed his fingers into the letter shin. According to Hebrew sources, the High Priest's hands were close to one another and formed five openings. Five is a Biblical number for grace, and the blessing was a picture of God's grace and favor being placed upon the people.

The letter shin is also important because the letter itself represents God's name. Orthodox Jews never attempt to pronounce the sacred name of God (Yahweh), but will instead say either the name *Adonai* or *HaShem*. The word HaShem, in Hebrew, means "the name." The letter shin is placed on an object called a mezuzah. This religious object is placed on the door posts of religious Jews around the world. It is a small flat or round object whose feature design on the outer shell is the letter shin. Inside each mezuzah is a place to insert a small, handwritten parchment with selected Scriptures from the book of Deuteronomy.

Not only does the shape of the mountains of Moriah and Zion form a Hebrew letter representing God's name, but the very topography of the peak of Mount Moriah itself also has a shape similar to the Hebrew letter yud. The letter yud is the tenth letter of the Hebrew alphabet, and it is the smallest letter of the twenty-two letters of the alphabet. When translating Hebrew to English, the letter yud becomes the letter J. The following important Biblical names begin with the letter yud: Joshua, Jacob, Judah, Jehovah, Jerusalem, and Jesus.

The true significance of the letter yud is again the sacred name of God. In English we say Jehovah, but the name in Hebrew is actually YHWH or Yahweh. The first Hebrew letter of this name is the letter yud. In Hebrew this letter represents a hand. The top part of Mount Moriah, where the Temple once stood, forms the letter yud. Indeed, the hand of the Lord did manifest in this place!

The mystery of why God chose Jerusalem continues when we ask ourselves, "Why did God choose Jerusalem as the location for the Messiah to be crucified? Once again, the thread of Eden continues to weave an astonishing pattern that is linked with the crucifixion of Christ.

CHAPTER 7

The Crucifixion and the Eden Connection

"Then delivered he him therefore unto them to be crucified. And they took Jesus, and led him away. And he bearing his cross went forth into a place called the place of a skull, which is called in the Hebrew Golgotha." – JOHN 19:16-17

The Heavenly Father had a plan from the foundation of the world. The Lamb of God would be slain and, through His ultimate sacrifice, the redemption of the world would be sealed (John 3:16). However, the site of the execution of God's final offering must be in the same place where the first king and priest lived, where Abraham offered Isaac, where Jacob's ladder was seen, and where Solomon's Temple once stood. Christ must die in Jerusalem.

I believe that Christ, the last Adam, redeemed mankind in the same place where the first Adam destroyed mankind's spiritual destiny. Through God's redemptive plan, men could once again enter the paradise of God, eat of the tree of life, and enjoy face-to-face fellowship with God.

The crucifixion of Jesus contains details that, to the casual reader, may hold little significance. But to the serious Bible student, the deeper clues unlock the mystery of the ages.

Cursing the Fig Tree

Several days before Christ's death, He saw a fig tree without fruit and cursed it. The next day the tree was dead. There are several theological opinions that attempt to explain why Christ cursed a fig tree when it was not the season for the trees to produce figs (Mark 11:13). Many suggest that, spiritually, the fig tree represented Israel, and that Christ was demonstrating how the nation would go under a curse for their unbelief. Israel is compared to a fig tree (Judges chapter 9 and Hosea 9:10). However, there is another possible explanation.

After Adam sinned, he and Eve hid among the trees in the garden and sewed fig leaves to hide their shame. The fig tree produces small green fruit before it produces the leaves and, as it matures, the large leaves cover and hide the fruit underneath it.

A few days after cursing the fig tree, Christ hung on a cross to bring salvation to the world. Christ cursed the fig tree as if to demonstrate how Adam attempted to cover his shame with fig leaves and hide among the fig trees. But mankind would no longer be able to hide their sins or their shame with an artificial man-made covering.

The area where Jesus cursed the fig tree was Bethphage, near Bethany (Mark 11:1-14). The name Bethphage is an Aramaic word that means "fig house." It was noted for its fig trees. This area is located near the Mount of Olives, which is the main mountain east of Jerusalem from which pilgrims can view Mount Moriah and the Temple Mount. If the tree of life was once upon the Temple Mount, and if Adam sinned at the tree of knowledge, then the area of the fig trees (near Bethphage) was within a short walking distance from the area of Adam's sin. According to Moses, both trees were in the same vicinity and were in the midst (center) of the garden (Genesis 2:9). The fig tree where Adam and Eve sought an artificial covering is parallel to the event of Christ cursing the fig tree near the Mount of Olives.

The Serpent with Legs

In the Genesis account, the serpent is an important part of the narrative. After man sinned, God placed a curse on the serpent when He said, "On your belly you will go…" The implication is that the serpent once moved by a method other than crawling on its belly. Researchers in Israel made a discovery several years ago which reveals that ancient serpents may have had legs.

According to secular researchers, snakes lived in the Jerusalem area one hundred million years ago. About a quarter of a century ago, several unusual and well-preserved snake fossils were discovered in a stone quarry in Ein Yabrud near Ramallah, which is in the West Bank area of Israel. These ancient fossils were serpents with two small hind legs. These snakes were considered the most primitive ever found. That discovery gives added credence to the verse in Genesis:

> *"And the LORD God said unto the serpent, Because thou hast done this, thou art cursed above all cattle, and above every beast of the field; upon thy belly shalt thou go, and dust shalt thou eat all the days of thy life."* – GENESIS 3:14

Apparently the serpent in those days was able to both communicate and walk on hind legs. Interestingly, these fossils were found in Israel, not far from Jerusalem. Again, a modern discovery near Jerusalem has a parallel to the Genesis account of the serpent in the garden.

The Trees in the Garden

Christ is called the last man Adam (1 Corinthians 15:45). The first man Adam was in the garden, and the last Adam entered a garden called Gethsemane (Matthew 26:36). The first Adam hid among the trees in the garden, and the last Adam interceded among the trees in Gethsemane (Matthew 26:39). The first Adam encountered the influence of the serpent and the last man Adam encountered the power of the old serpent, as Satan put pressure on Christ and almost caused Him to die before He could complete His assignment. Paul mentioned this in Hebrews:

> "Who, in the days of His flesh, when He had offered up prayers and supplications, with vehement cries and tears to Him who was able to save Him from death, and was heard because of His godly fear, though He was a Son, yet He learned obedience by the things which He suffered." – HEBREWS 5:7-9 (NKJV)

The first Adam was told that the earth would bring forth thorns and thistles and Adam would sweat to make his bread. The second Adam experienced sweat as it became great drops of blood (Luke 22:44). Later the second Adam, Jesus, would have a crown of thorns cutting the tender flesh of His forehead. Each aspect of Adam's fall in the garden correlates to the sufferings of Christ: both were in a garden, both encountered Satan, both dealt with thorns, and both experienced sweat.

The Hill of the Skull

The name of the site of Christ's crucifixion is mentioned in the four gospels, but three different names are used: the hill of a skull, Calvary, and Golgotha. Calvary was the Latin name and Golgotha was the Hebrew name. The Jews would have used the Hebrew name and the Roman soldiers the Latin name.

> *"And when they were come to the place, which is called Calvary, there they crucified him, and the malefactors, one on the right hand, and the other on the left."* –LUKE 23:33

> *"And he bearing his cross went forth into a place called the place of a skull, which is called in the Hebrew Golgotha."* –JOHN 19:17

There are several theories as to why this hill was called the hill of the skull. Some suggest that there are certain features on the hill which appear in the form of a human skull. These features are pointed out to tourists who visit Gordon's Calvary, a beautiful garden on the north side of Jerusalem, just outside the Damascus Gate. Unearthed in 1867, it was noted by British General Charles Gordon who was admiring the landscape around Jerusalem when he noticed a hill that, to his imagination, looked like a large skull. Today, the Garden Tomb Association has preserved the area near the hill where an ancient tomb, a winepress, and evidence of an ancient garden is revealed. Tourists are shown the hill and an old picture that looks remarkably similar to the top part of a large skull. This site is affectionately referred to as the Protestant site.

Catholic and Greek Orthodox leaders argue against the historical accuracy of this site. They believe the crucifixion location is the present-day site of the Church of the Holy Sepulcher. This church is located within the old city of Jerusalem. The mother of Constantine marked this area in the middle of the fourth century, and later a church was built to commemorate the crucifixion event. Most of what tourists see today is the work of the Crusaders who, in the year 1149, built a huge basilica over the traditional site of Calvary and the tomb of Christ. This location is revered by Catholics, Greek Orthodox, Armenians, Coptic Christians, Syrian Orthodox, and Ethiopians who share the location.

Which is correct? Further research seems to indicate that the hill of the skull could be the actual site of the crucifixion. Both Christian and Jewish traditions teach that Adam was buried in this area after his death. Jewish tradition says that Noah, before entering the ark, took the skull of Adam with him and later gave it to Shem (Melchizedek) who took it to Jerusalem and buried it. The early Christians knew this tradition and some believed that, when Christ was crucified, His blood ran down the cross and into a crack where Adam's skull was buried. Interestingly, many Medieval and Renaissance artists paint the crucifixion with a skull at the base of the cross. Origin, an early church father (185 – 253 A.D.) stated in the second century that Calvary received its name because the skull of Adam was found there. According to early church tradition, the first man Adam was buried in Jerusalem at the same place where the last Adam was to be buried! Considering the patterns and parallels of history, I would not be surprised if Adam was buried in the place where Jesus was crucified.

The hill of the skull is also linked to the ancient giants that once roamed the earth. In David's time, there were five giants living in the Promised Land. They were Goliath, Lahmi, Ishbibanob, Saph, and the giant from Gath (1 Samuel 17:4; 2 Samuel 21:15-22). David and his mighty men slew the remnants of giants in the earth, thus destroying the seed of the serpent (Genesis 3:15). After slaying Goliath, David took the giant's sword and beheaded him (1 Samuel 17:51). Keep in mind that the site of Christ's crucifixion was called Golgotha in the Hebrew language.

In King David's time, there were five giants in Israel. David slew Goliath from Gath (1 Samuel 17:51). David cut off the head of Goliath and the Bible says that he carried the head to Jerusalem (1 Samuel 17:54).

The hill of the crucifixion is called the hill of the skull, but the question is, "Whose skull?" Could the Hebrew name, Golgotha, be a form of the name Goliath from Gath, or Gol-gath-a? If so, this is a dynamic picture of David defeating the natural seed of the serpents (the giants), and of Jesus defeating the spiritual seed of the serpent through His death and resurrection! This theory would fulfill the promise that God gave in Genesis:

> "And the LORD God said unto the serpent, Because thou hast done this, thou art cursed above all cattle, and above every beast of the field; upon thy belly shalt thou go, and dust shalt thou eat all the days of thy life: And I will put enmity between thee and the woman, and between thy seed and her seed; it shall bruise thy head, and thou shalt bruise his heel." – GENESIS 3:14-15

If the giants that once roamed the earth were indeed the seed of the serpent, and since David and his men removed the final traces of giants (1 Chronicles 20:1-8), then David destroyed the natural seed of the serpent. At His crucifixion, Christ hung on Golgotha where His feet were positioned above the skull of one of the most feared giants in history.*

God revealed the promise of redemption to Adam before he was expelled from the garden. If the theory of Jerusalem being the center of the garden is correct, this means that God announced the judgment of the serpent in the same area where the redemption of mankind one day would be provided. Perhaps this is why David brought the skull of Goliath over eighteen miles to Jerusalem from the Valley of Elah (1 Samuel 17:19). David knew something would happen on that mountain, just as Abraham, centuries before David, understood that "in the Mount of the Lord it shall be seen" (Genesis 22:14).

The Mount of Olives Site

If you have ever traveled to the Holy Land, you know the power of tradition. Entire tourist sites are built around a tradition, and there is no shortage of Catholic and Orthodox churches to mark the site of the stories in the Bible. The same is true with the crucifixion site. More recently, a third interesting theory has emerged. It was first introduced by Ernest Martin, Ph.D., in a book entitled *Secrets of Golgotha.* Using sacred and secular history, along with New Testament word studies, Dr. Martin suggests that there is Biblical and historical evidence to indicate that the site of the crucifixion may be a high knoll on the Mount of Olives, which is located on the east side of Jerusalem, just outside the eastern wall of the Temple Mount. One noted Israeli archeologist told me that he was very impressed with Dr. Martin's detailed and scholarly research. While the idea of a Mount of Olives crucifixion site departs radically from the standard traditions, there are several interesting points that could validate Dr. Martin's theory.

In the 1873 edition of the *Palestinian Quarterly,* a Dr. Hutchinson suggested that the crucifixion of Jesus may have taken place on the east side of the Temple Mount, which would place it somewhere on the Mount of Olives.

The Mount of Olives and the Red Heifer

The Mount of Olives is linked to a mystical sacrifice called the sacrifice of the red heifer. Moses recorded the procedure for this special offering in the book of Numbers:

> *"This is the ordinance of the law which the LORD hath commanded, saying, Speak unto the children of Israel, that they bring thee a red*

heifer without spot, wherein is no blemish, and upon which never came yoke: And ye shall give her unto Eleazar the priest, that he may bring her forth without the camp, and one shall slay her before his face: And Eleazar the Priest shall take of her blood with his finger, and sprinkle of her blood directly before the tabernacle of the congregation seven times: And one shall burn the heifer in his sight; her skin, and her flesh, and her blood, with her dung, shall he burn: And the priest shall take cedar wood, and hyssop, and scarlet, and cast it into the midst of the burning of the heifer. Then the priest shall wash his clothes, and he shall bathe his flesh in water, and afterward he shall come into the camp, and the priest shall be unclean until the even."

—NUMBERS 19:2-7

The sacrifice of the red heifer was a perfect preview of the crucifixion of Christ. The red heifer was a female sacrifice and all other offerings were male. This could allude to the fact that, through Christ's death, He purchased for Himself a bride (Revelation 21:2 and 9). Through Christ's death and resurrection, He would birth and build His church (Matthew 16:18). The Greek word for church is *ekklesia* and is a feminine Greek word, referring to those who are called out to join the assembly.

The sacrificial red heifer was taken outside the camp to be offered, just as Christ was taken outside the gate of the city to be crucified (Hebrews 13:12). Cedar wood was tossed in a fire as the heifer was burning, and Christ was crucified on a wooden cross (John 19:17). A branch of a hyssop plant was tossed into the fire as the fire consumed the heifer, and as Christ hung dying on the cross, hyssop with vinegar was placed to His mouth (John 19:29). Scarlet colored threads were thrown into the burning flames, and a scarlet robe was placed on Christ's shoulders (Matthew 27:28). The priest looked on as the heifer was burning, and the priest stood at the cross watching as Christ died (John 19:21).

The Jewish Mishna gives further details about the laws of burning the red heifer. As the priest cut the throat of the heifer, he would catch the blood of the heifer in his right hand, dip the fingers of his left hand into his right hand, and sprinkle the blood by pointing to the door of the Tabernacle (later the Temple) seven times. The right hand can allude to the Jews and the left hand to the Gentiles. This priestly action painted a beautiful picture of Christ's blood initiating a new covenant with the Jews, and how that later, the Gentiles were grafted in, giving them access to enter the heavenly Temple to enjoy forgiveness and God's Presence. Just as the priest dipped his fingers seven times into the sacrificial blood, so Christ shed His blood seven times on His body during His sufferings.

Times that Christ Shed His blood	Location of the shedding
His sweat became as drops of blood (Luke 22:44)	His face
They placed a crown of thorns on His head (John 19:2)	His head
A nail was driven into His right hand (Luke 24:39-40)	His right hand
A nail was driven into His left hand (Luke 24:39-40)	His left hand
A nail was driven into His right foot (Luke 24:39-40	His right foot
A nail was driven into His left foot (Luke 24:39-40)	His left foot
A spear pierced His side (John 19:34)	His side

Just as sprinkling the blood of the red heifer seven times was symbolic of completion, so was the shedding of Christ's blood seven times a picture of the completed work of redemption.

After Jerusalem became the capital of ancient Israel and the Temple was built, the sacrifice of the red heifer occurred on the Mount of Olives. The priest sacrificed the heifer about midway up the Mount of Olives and could see the entrance to the Holy Place by looking over the top of the eastern wall of Jerusalem. Because the red heifer was sacrificed on the Mount of Olives and is a picture of the crucifixion of Jesus, some suggest that Christ dying on the Mount of Olives fits the pattern.

From the Mount of Olives

The gospel writers give a series of facts related to the crucifixion of Christ:

- He was led outside the city walls (John 19:16 and Hebrews 13:12)

- He was crucified on a hill called Golgotha (Luke 23:33)

- The site was located near a garden (John 19:41)

- The site was located near burial tombs (John 19:41)

- The tomb of Christ was owned by a rich man (Matthew 27:59-60)

- The tomb was cut out of the rock on the hill (Matthew 27:59-60)

- The Centurion could see the Temple veil (Matthew 27:54)

- The Centurion saw the rocks rent and the veil torn (Matthew 27:51-54)

Outside the City Walls

In summary, there are two traditional sites in Jerusalem that are identified as possible locations for Christ's crucifixion: the Church of the Holy Sepulcher, which has been the designated site for over 1,660 years, and Gordon's Calvary, now called the Garden Tomb. We don't know for certain the exact location of the crucifixion, but one thing is certain. The place of His crucifixion, burial, and resurrection could not have been located within the walls of the city of Jerusalem. It was against Jewish law to have a cemetery within the confines of the city. The carcass of a dead body made the ground unclean and the Law of Moses demanded that a person who touched anything dead was unclean until evening and needed to wash in water for ritualistic purification (Numbers chapter 19). It would have been necessary for Christ's execution to occur outside of the walls of Jerusalem.

The Bible indicates that Christ was crucified outside the gate (Hebrews 13:12). This is one of the main arguments against the true location being the Church of the Holy Sepulcher. Many scholars believe that this location is within the old wall of Jerusalem from the Roman period. Portions of this wall are still buried underground.

Christ was charged with blasphemy against God and against the Temple. Christ said, "Destroy this Temple and in three days I will build it back again." The ignorant religious leaders alleged that Christ was threatening to destroy the physical Jewish Temple (John 2:19). Jesus, however, was speaking about His own physical body, which would be beaten beyond recognition and raised back to life on the third day (John 2:21-22). Since Christ was charged with the unpardonable sin of blasphemy (Matthew 26:65), His execution should have been by stoning:

"Then the LORD said to Moses: Take the blasphemer outside the camp.

All those who heard him are to lay their hands on his head, and the entire assembly is to stone him." — LEVITICUS 24:13-15

In Exodus there is an account of a young man whose mother was Jewish and whose father was an Egyptian. The young man was caught cursing God's name, and he was sentenced to death by stoning (Leviticus 24:11-14). Jewish law taught that a blasphemer was to be executed outside the camp (Numbers 15:35) and in the face of God.

The Face of God and the Gate

The Mount of Olives now comes into the picture. In Moses' time, the face of God alluded to the eastern side of the Tabernacle and, specifically, to a curtain where the priest and people entered into the outer court of the Tabernacle. This point can also be born out in the Temple Scroll, an ancient scroll discovered at Qumran and translated by Professor Yadin. According to Yadin, the scroll mentions that any person who had defilements and could not enter the city must remain to the east of the sanctuary. In Jerusalem, the east would be the Mount of Olives. This may also be the reason why the special sin offerings—such as the red heifer—were sacrificed outside the camp on the east side.

In Jerusalem is a deep gorge called the Kidron Valley, which separates the Mount of Olives from the Temple Mount platform. In Scripture this valley is called the "Valley of Jehoshaphat." In Hebrew the name means "the valley where God judges." There are at least fourteen Christian sources which state that this valley will be the area where God will one day judge the nations (Joel 3:2).

During Christ's time, if you were to stand on the peak of the Mount of Olives, which is located to the east of Mount Moriah (Zechariah 14:4), and look westward, you would be looking directly at the Eastern Gate.

Above the city wall would be the two large doors to the front entrance of the Temple. This view can be seen *only* from the Mount of Olives. If a person were to be crucified in the area of the Church of the Holy Sepulcher, the people of the city would see only the back retaining wall and a portion of the upper back part of the Temple where the veil was located. If Christ were crucified from Gordon's Calvary site, the right side of the Temple complex (and not the main entrance or door of the Holy Place) would be visible.

Because the Centurion at the cross felt the earthquake and saw the veil being torn and the rocks rent, he was convinced that Jesus was the Son of God (Mark 15:39). The only position on any hill which could enable a person to see the torn veil would be from the Mount of Olives, when the two large doors to the Temple were opened.

The crucifixion site is linked to the word head or skull. In the Hebrew language, the word for head is the word *rosh*. For example, the Jewish Feast of Trumpets is called Rosh Hashanah, which means "the head of the year." Forty days after His resurrection, Christ ascended back to heaven from the top of the Mount of Olives, near Bethany (Luke 24:50-51). In Hebrew, the top area of the Mount of Olives would be considered the head, or *rosh* of the mountain. This is confirmed in the Biblical account of David fleeing the city of Jerusalem when his son was threatening to assassinate him. We read:

> *"And David went up by the ascent of Mount Olivet, and wept as he went up, and had his head covered, and he went barefoot: and all the people that was with him covered every man his head, and they went up, weeping as they went up."* — 2 SAMUEL 15:30

Two verses later, David came to the top of the mount and worshipped God (2 Samuel 15:32). The Hebrew word for top is *rosh*. Since the word *rosh* means "head", and *Golgotha* means the "hill of the skull," is this another link revealing that the location of the crucifixion is on the peak or top of the hill itself, and not at the base of the hill as some suggest? If we consider the possibility that Christ may have been crucified at the top of the Mount of Olives overlooking the city, then the cross would be sitting on the rosh of the hill, or on the top and the head.

We know from the gospel accounts that Christ was crucified near a garden and near a new tomb. The tomb belonged to one of Christ's secret followers, a wealthy Jew named Joseph of Arimathaea. The crucifixion site and the tomb were in the same location, according to Scripture:

> *"In the place where he was crucified, there was a garden and in the garden a new tomb..."* – JOHN 19:41

Tombs and Gardens on the Mount of Olives

The garden tomb in Jerusalem is a beautiful setting for remembering the Lord's death and resurrection. No doubt it was an ancient garden area. Is there any evidence that both tombs and gardens were also located on the Mount of Olives? If not, the evidence stops here. If so, there is another possible piece of the puzzle.

At the base of the Mount of Olives lies the famous Garden of Gethsemane. The Bible says that Christ would visit there often as a place for prayer. This is the same garden where he prayed all night before his illegal arrest (Matthew 26:36). The garden lies between the Mount of Olives and the Eastern Gate, and it is separated by the deep ravine of the Kidron Valley. This garden was and still is known for its olive trees, flowers, and beauty.

Halfway up the Mount of Olives, archeologists discovered a very large burial complex dating back to the Roman period, or the time of Christ.

Many stone boxes called ossuaries were discovered in the niches cut into the limestone rock. There is also a large underground burial chamber owned by an Arab family and located on the Mount of Olives. It is called the tomb of the prophets. In early times, the name of the prophet Zechariah was discovered above one of the tomb's entrances. This is the same name of the prophet who prophesied that the Messiah would return to the Mount of Olives (Zechariah 14:4).

Among the ossuaries, archeologists have also discovered small bits of pottery and coins that date back as early as 45 AD. The bones buried in this location were placed in these stone carved boxes within fifteen years of Christ's crucifixion, meaning that this area was a graveyard in the time of Christ. Even the Biblical names of Mary, Martha, and Lazarus have been discovered etched on several ancient ossuaries.

Today, the lower southern section of the Mount of Olives is covered with thousands of Jewish graves. Many Jewish people prize this location for burial, with the belief that when the Messiah returns to the Mount of Olives, they will be raised and will follow the Messiah into the city of Jerusalem.

Evidence indicates that the Mount of Olives has both the gardens and the tombs required in the crucifixion story. Joseph of Arimathaea, the rich man who owned the tomb that Christ borrowed, was also a member of the Jewish Sanhedrin. May I suggest that a person of his stature would have his burial site on the second most important mountain outside of Mount Moriah, which would be the Mount of Olives? Today the Mount of Olives is the most expensive cemetery in the world in which to be buried. Even in ancient times, only the rich could have afforded to be buried there, and Joseph of Arimathaea was a very rich man (Matthew 27:57).

Outside the Gate

Both the bull and the red heifer were offered outside the camp. In Moses' time, this was the outskirts of the Tabernacle and the tents where the people dwelt, usually on the eastern side and about two thousand cubits from the Tabernacle itself (Mishna, Tracate Parah). Paul indicated that Christ was offered outside the gate (Hebrews 13:12). In Christ's time, the entrances to Jerusalem were through the city gates. There were several main gates leading into the city. Today they are called:

Name of Gate	Location of Gate
The Eastern Gate	built on the east
The Damascus Gate	built on the north
The Dung Gate	built on the west
The Saint Stephens Gate	built on the east
The Double Gates	built on the south
The Triple Gates	built on the south

The only gate on the eastern wall that was the main gate into the Temple is the Eastern Gate, also called the golden gate and the "gate called beautiful" (Acts 3:10). This gate was called, "the gate of the Temple" in Acts 3:2. In the Greek language it says *the* gate and not *a* gate. In Greek, the word *the* is a definite article identifying the importance of this gate to the Temple. Hebrew scholars believe that in Christ's time, there was a three-tiered ramp that led from the center of the Mount of Olives to the front of the Eastern Gate. It was built so that worshippers entering the Temple would not be defiled by the bones of a carcass buried in the

Kidron Valley. The priests also led the red heifer across this ramp to be offered on the Mount of Olives. Christ rode on a donkey and used this ramp to enter the eastern entrance of the Temple (Matthew 21:7-10). This also would have been the ramp that the priest used to lead Jesus to the top of the Mount of Olives to be crucified, assuming this is the site of the crucifixion.

The Centurion Saw These Things

From the Mount of Olives, when the doors to the Temple were opened, a person could have seen the large Temple veil. Since the crucifixion was near the time of Passover, the two large doors of the Temple would have been opened and a person could have viewed the famous veil with the cherubim. According to the Jewish Talmud, in the second Temple (in Christ's day) there were two veils, with a cubit space between them (Yoma 5:1). The main veil was woven in white, gold, purple, blue, and scarlet—the same colors found in the veil in the Tabernacle of Moses (Exodus 26:31).

The Bible indicates that when Jesus said, "It is finished," three major things transpired. First, an earthquake shook the entire region (Matthew 27:54). Second, the rocks were split, including many of the tombs (Matthew 27:51-53). And third, the huge veil in the Temple was ripped from top to bottom (Matthew 27:51-53).

According to Jewish sources, this veil was thirty feet across and forty feet high. It consisted of seventy-two squares which were woven together by women at the Temple in the Chamber of the Curtain. Two new veils were made each year (Shekalim 8:5). The veil was a hand's breadth thick to ensure that it would not tear. A team of oxen were used to attempt to rip it, and they failed. Yet, at the crucifixion of Christ, the veil was ripped in half from the top to bottom (Matthew 27:51). The spiritual explanation is that the Hand of God severed the veil to once again allow mankind access into His Holy Presence!

The natural explanation given for the torn veil is that the large beam in the center of the roof of the Temple split as a result of the earthquake, thus ripping the veil in two parts. As the earth quaked, the stones split, and the veil was ripped, a Roman Centurion at the foot of the cross became a believer in Christ. It was what he saw that convinced him:

"And behold, the veil of the temple was rent in twain from the top to the bottom; and the earth did quake, and the rocks rent; And the graves were opened; and many bodies of the saints which slept arose, And came out of the graves after his resurrection, and went into the holy city, and appeared unto many. Now when the centurion, and they that were with him, watching Jesus, saw the earthquake, and those things that were done, they feared greatly, saying, Truly this was the Son of God." – MATTHEW 27:51-54

Notice that it says, "…when he saw these *things*." These things were those events surrounding the earthquake: the rocks being split and the veil being torn. For this centurion to witness the ripping of the Temple veil, he must have been standing near the top of the Mount of Olives. From this vantage point, the hardened Roman soldier could have felt the earthquake and viewed the confusion on the Temple Mount as the stunned priest saw the mighty veil of separation torn asunder. Imagine the shock to those present that, at the same moment Christ spoke His last words, the earth shook and the veil was torn!

Jewish sages have written that, at the most, twelve red heifers were offered throughout Israel's history. Because the red heifer was slain and burnt on a specific area on the Mount of Olives, and because this special offering was a picture of the crucifixion, the location of the heifers' death may be another indicator of the connection between the Mount of Olives and Christ's own death.

The Early Church Worshipped on this Site

Approximately forty years after the resurrection of Christ, the Roman tenth legion invaded Jerusalem and burned the Temple, eventually toppling the stones to remove the freshly melted gold from the surface. In 71 AD, the Romans plowed the city under with salt so that nothing would grow in the area in the future. From that moment, the Jews were scattered. Many of the Holy sites were eventually forgotten and the locations lost through centuries of desolation.

Although the city lay in ruins, for many centuries it was common for Christian pilgrims who traveled through the Holy Land to ascend to Jerusalem and pray at the former location of the Holy City. Early Christian historians reveal that the Christians would stop at a certain place on the Mount of Olives, read Scripture, and pray.

Before the time of Emperor Constantine, early historical writings indicate that Christian pilgrims who traveled to Jerusalem would worship from the top of the Mount of Olives in a cave near the summit. This information is found in the writings of Eusebius, the first Christian historian (Proof of the Gospel, VI.18). Dr. Peter Michas suggests that the cave and the tombs that were the focal point of the pilgrim's activity may be the tombs that are located near The Church of the Pater Noster on the Mount of Olives.

The Summary

It was necessary for Christ to be crucified in Jerusalem for several reasons:

1. **Jerusalem is the city where God placed His name.** It was and is the City of God and the Mountain of the Lord.

2. **Jerusalem is the place where Abraham offered Isaac.** The binding of Isaac in Genesis chapter 22 has all of the parallels to the crucifixion of Christ. The Savior needed to die and be raised in the same place where God confirmed His covenant with Abraham.

3. **Jerusalem is the place where Melchizedek ruled.** Christ's heavenly ministry is after the order of the Melchizedek priesthood. This first king and priest of the Most High had his headquarters in Jerusalem; therefore, the new Priesthood of Christ must begin in Jerusalem, in the same area where the original Melchizedek ruled.

4. **Only Jerusalem could fulfill the types and shadows of the law.** The red heifer sacrifice had several prophetic parallels that point to the crucifixion of Christ. Our Savior did not come to destroy the law but to fulfill it. Since the red heifer was offered in Jerusalem from the Mount of Olives, outside the gate, so was Christ offered in Jerusalem from the same area outside the gate.

5. **Christ had to restore man's access back to God.** Adam's sin was passed from generation to generation. Only the High Priest could enter the sacred Holy of Holies once a year to atone for Israel's sin. Christ came to the very area of the Temple to restore man's access back to God.

6. Christ had to restore Eden. The second man Adam—Jesus Christ—came to the area of the original Garden of Eden and restored eternal life back to man!

*IF YOU WISH TO STUDY MORE DETAILED INFORMATION ABOUT THE ANCIENT GIANTS AND THEIR LINK TO THE SEED OF THE SERPENT, SEE PERRY'S STONE'S VIDEO (OR DVD) ENTITLED *The Mystery of Fallen Angels, Giants and Evil Spirits.* TO UNDERSTAND MORE ABOUT THE LINK BETWEEN GOLIATH AND GOLGOTHA, READ PERRY'S BOOK, *The Mystery of the Priesthood and the Blood.*

CHAPTER 8

The Final Battle for Eden:
Satan's Hatred for the Jews and Jerusalem

"And when the dragon saw that he was cast unto the earth, he persecuted the woman which brought forth the man child." –REVELATION 12:13

One of the final global conflicts initiated by Satan will involve the nation of Israel and the Jewish people. This spiritual struggle, found in Revelation chapter 12, will be unleashed on the earth when the old ancient serpent, Satan, is expelled from his command center in the second heaven and cast down to the earth in the middle of the seven-year tribulation (Revelation 12:9). Satan could not exalt himself above the throne of God in the heavenly Temple, and he failed to rule the paradise of God in heaven. Satan's assignment was to gain access to the earthly garden and spread his claws of iniquity around the world. At the conclusion of time, the battle will end where it all began—in Jerusalem.

Why have the Jews experienced more persecution than any other ethnic group? From the slavery in Egypt, to the dividing of the tribes by the Assyrians, to the destruction of the two Temples and Jerusalem by the Babylonians and the Romans, the Jews have been persecuted and slain for centuries. The inquisition and the holocaust cost over six million lives. Why does Satan hate the Jews? There are several reasons:

1. **The Jews had the only true covenant with the one true God.** In Abraham's day the nations had turned to idolatry. Abraham received a revelation of the true God and entered into an everlasting covenant with the Almighty, with circumcision being the token of the covenant (Genesis 17:11).

    Every male descendant of Abraham, at eight days of age, was to be circumcised according to Genesis 17:12. Abraham's son Isaac, and his son Jacob and his twelve sons, formed the nation of Israel. They were "marked men" who were required to remain faithful to God's covenant or else be cut off from among the people. Thus, the only nation to worship the true God and enter into an everlasting covenant was the nation of Hebrew people.

2. **The Jews built on earth what was originally built in heaven.** The covenant with Abraham gave God legal rights to work through the Hebrew nation. God's desire was to dwell among His people. Moses received the Divine revelation to construct a Tabernacle that was patterned after the Temple of God in heaven (Hebrews 8:5). The portable tent included sacred furniture, similar to the sacred furniture in heaven, including the Ark of the Testimony (Revelation 11:19), the golden altar (Revelation 8:3), and even the golden candlestick (Revelation 1:12). The wilderness Tabernacle and the Jerusalem Temples gave God direct access to man on the Day of Atonement. Imagine Satan's anger to see how the Jews built on earth what was built in heaven—a place for God to dwell among His people.

3. **The Jews carried the Word of God.** Paul spoke of the Hebrew people and asked the question, "What profit has a Jew?" He then answered, "Much in every way! Chiefly because to them was committed the oracles of God" (Romans 3:2). The word "oracles" refers to the utterances of God, or the words of God. God first revealed the Torah (the first five books of the Bible) to Moses, then the Psalms and the Prophets. The prophets and writers of the Holy Scripture were Hebrew people. While the surrounding nations sought wisdom from deaf and mute idols made of clay and stone, the Hebrew God was a Spirit who manifested through wind, fire, glory clouds, and burning bushes.

4. **The Jews brought forth the Messiah.** The Savior of the world, Jesus Christ, was conceived of the Holy Spirit in the womb of a Jewish woman named Mary. She married a young man named Joseph, who was a Jewish male from the lineage of the house of David (Luke 1:27). Christ was from a Jewish family, lived in a Jewish home, studied the Torah in Jewish schools, and attended Jewish synagogue (Mark 1:29). Christ also celebrated the three feasts that all Jewish males were required to attend (Exodus 23:17). He participated in the Feast of Dedication which was Hanukkah (John 10:22). God chose the Hebrew nation to bring forth the Redeemer of the world.

5. **Jerusalem would be the future city of the Messiah.** Jerusalem is a city with a mysterious and amazing past and a wonderful future. The Holy City will one day become the spiritual and political capital of the entire world when the Messiah returns to rule on earth for one thousand years (Revelation 19:15 and 20:2-7). The one thousand year reign of Christ will initiate extreme and powerful changes in the earth, including the governments, the animal kingdom, and the

increase of Jerusalem.

The prophet Ezekiel released a vision that depicted the future millennial Temple in Jerusalem. The King (Jesus) will rule the nations with a rod of iron from His throne which will sit in the Holy Place of the Temple.

From the tree of life, to the Ark of the Covenant, to the throne of the King, the Mountain of the Lord was marked from the beginning of creation.

6. **The Jews and Jerusalem proved that the Bible is true.** When God swore an oath to Abraham and forged a covenant for the land of Israel and for the Hebrew nation, the Almighty could "swear by no one higher so he swore by himself" (Hebrews 6:13). This statement implies that God would be so faithful to His covenant that if He broke His words to Abraham, He would remove Himself from His throne in heaven. Since the initiation of this covenant, Satan has attempted to destroy the Jews, Jerusalem, and Israel because the existence of these three proves the truth of God's Word and reveals the faithfulness of God to His covenant.

No prophecy relating to the return of Christ could have come to pass until Israel was again a nation and Jerusalem was controlled by the Jewish people. Last-day Biblical prophecies related to the return and reign of Messiah began to come to pass after Israel was re-birthed and after Jerusalem was again in Jewish hands.

If Satan could destroy Israel, Jerusalem, or the Jewish people, he could prove God's Word a lie and win the battle by default. The final battle before the King Messiah returns will be over Jerusalem and will center on Jerusalem. It is called Armageddon. I picture this battle as the last assault on Eden.

CHAPTER 9

The Final Restoration of Eden

"Blessed and holy is he who has part in the first resurrection. Over such the second death has no power, but they shall be priests of God and of Christ, and shall reign with Him a thousand years."

— REVELATION 20:6

In the future, God is going to restore the glory of fellowship of the ancient Garden of Eden with the entire world. This glorious event will begin at the return of Jesus Christ to rule and reign from the city of Jerusalem for one thousand years. The second Adam, Jesus Christ, will exercise dominion over the earth as the first Adam did before his fall. Jerusalem will be the headquarters of the world and Christ will be the King (Revelation 19:16).

Christ ministered, worshipped, died, and was raised in Jerusalem. After being seen alive for forty days after His resurrection, He ascended back to the Father from the Mount of Olives (Acts 1:11-12). From 70

AD, for over eighteen hundred years, Israel was nonexistent as a Jewish nation. Jerusalem was a poor city which changed hands with the rise and fall of empires and world leaders. In 1517, The Ottoman Turks rebuilt the walls of the old city of Jerusalem. Four hundred years later the British took Jerusalem from the Turks and, in 1948, the United Nations voted to recognize the state of Israel.

During the Six Day War in 1967, Israeli paratroopers seized the eastern section of Jerusalem, which included the Mount of Olives, the Kidron Valley, and the Temple Mount. Two Islamic mosques have been erected on the Temple Mount—the Dome of the Rock and Al Aqsa. The Israelis feared that annexing the mountain into total Israeli control would incite another war with surrounding Muslim nations. The keys to the gate of the Temple compound were turned over to the head of the Islamic leadership in Jerusalem.

Today, Jerusalem is a modern city housing millions of citizens and hosting three major religions: Judaism, Christianity, and Islam. The Psalms reveal that, when the Lord shall build up Zion, then He shall appear in His glory (Psalm 102:16). Jerusalem has been and always will be the important key to the door of the prophetic future. Jerusalem has a magnificent future. During the coming one thousand year reign of Christ, the Lord will begin a process of restoring the communion and fellowship of the garden back to mankind!

The Lost River of Eden

As stated earlier in the book, the original Garden of Eden had one main river that parted into four heads. This unknown and unnamed river eventually disappeared or wove its way underground. One of the first changes at the beginning of the millennial reign will be the unleashing of a vast water source from under Jerusalem.

Christ will return to the Mount of Olives and cause the mountain to split into two halves:

> *"And in that day His feet will stand on the Mount of Olives, which faces Jerusalem on the east. And the Mount of Olives shall be split in two, from east to west, making a very large valley; Half of the mountain shall move toward the north, and half of it toward the south."* —ZECHARIAH 14:4 (NKJV)

The Mount of Olives sits directly in front of the Eastern Gate in Jerusalem. Zechariah said that, when the mountain splits, living waters will flow:

> *"And in that day it shall be that living waters shall flow from Jerusalem, half of them toward the eastern sea and half of them toward the western sea; in both summer and winter it shall occur."* —ZECHARIAH 14:8

As the mountain divides, the underground water source will release huge amounts of water that will flow into both the Mediterranean Sea and the Dead Sea. The Mediterranean is called the former sea and the Dead Sea is the hinder sea in Zechariah's prophecy. The earthquake will also shake the land near the Dead Sea—the location of the large underground source of water. The combination of the living water from Jerusalem and the water near the edge of the Dead Sea will cause the salty, lifeless Dead Sea to live and produce freshwater fish (Ezekiel 47:9).

Ezekiel describes these Jerusalem waters as flowing ankle deep from under the threshold of the Temple. A thousand cubits out they become knee deep, and another thousand cubits out they become waist deep. Eventually the waters become a river in which man can swim (Ezekiel 47:3-5). These waters bring healing to the Dead Sea, causing special trees to grow on either side of the river.

"Along the bank of the river, on this side and that, will grow all kinds of trees used for food; their leaves will not wither, and their fruit will not fail. They will bear fruit every month, because their water flows from the sanctuary. Their fruit will be for food, and their leaves for medicine." –Ezekiel 47:12 (NKJV)

The trees mentioned in this prophecy are unique. The fruit will be for food, and the trees will bear fruit during the twelve months of the year. The living waters from Jerusalem will have such a supernatural effect upon the trees that the very leaves on these trees will be used for medicine. These trees are similar to what we read about the tree of life in the heavenly Jerusalem. In Hebrew, the phrase "living waters" that was used by Ezekiel comes from a root word *chayah*, which means to nourish, preserve, and quicken.

The parallels between the heavenly river of life and the earthly living water, and the parallels between the heavenly tree of life and the trees growing on the banks of the living waters are unmistakable. The only difference is that the tree in the garden would have kept Adam alive forever had he partaken of its fruit continually, while those in earthly bodies who survive the tribulation and are still living during the millennial reign will eventually die. It appears that they will need healing, and the leaves on the trees will provide that healing. The Bible indicates that these survivors during the future millennium will live to be very old—and if they die before the age of one hundred, it will be rare (Isaiah 65:20). The Septuagint (the Old Testament translated into Greek) renders the passage, "Nor shall there be any more an untimely birth, and an old man who has not filled up his time." With Satan being bound and righteousness prevailing, health will again be restored to the earthly inhabitants who rule with Christ during the millennial reign.

In the heavenly city there is a river of water of life that proceeds from out of the throne of God and appears to flow throughout the Holy City (Revelation 22:1). During the Millennium, the living waters will flow from under the threshold of the altar in the newly erected Temple of the Messiah!

May I suggest that, if the theory of Jerusalem being the center of the garden is correct, the underground water source that will one day be unleashed in Jerusalem may be the lost river of Eden that once flowed through the entire garden? It would originate somewhere in the area of Turkey or Armenia with the headwaters of the Euphrates and the Tigris, travel through Israel, go south toward Egypt, and eventually link with the Nile (the ancient Gihon of Eden).

Just as the rivers of Eden supplied water—along with a mist from under the ground, according to Genesis 2:6—the future living water will restore the trees to the desert places and bring restoration of fresh water to the Dead Sea. The Lord will bring about a restitution of all things that Satan attempted to destroy during the 6,000 years of man's earthly governments.

The End is the Beginning

For many years I have preached that the things which have been are the things which shall be (Ecclesiastes 1:9-10). In the first two chapters of Genesis, everything is perfect. And in the final two chapters of Revelation, everything is perfect. This is because all things are going to end the same way they began. In the beginning there was no sin, and in the end there is no sin. In the beginning there was no pain, and in the end there is no pain. In the beginning there was no death, and in the end death is removed. In the beginning God walked with man in the garden, and in the end God will talk with man in the heavenly city. There was an earthly Eden (Genesis 2:8) and there was a heavenly Eden (Ezekiel 28:13).

The end will be the beginning! The earthly Jerusalem is a reflection of the heavenly Jerusalem, and the earthly Eden is a picture of the Paradise of God in heaven. This miracle of eternal life was wrought when the second Adam descended to the place of the first Adam's defeat and took on the serpent in a garden—the Garden of Gethsemane. Just as thorns were part of the curse placed upon the first Adam, the second Adam, Jesus Christ, had a crown of thorns pressed upon his head.

At His death the veil was torn and man was once again given access to the Holy of Holies and the eternal tree of life; except the tree of life was no longer a natural tree with twelve types of fruit, but was the tree called the cross, with fruit that would come from the revelation given to twelve disciples who would preach the message of eternal life in the cross of Christ!

The cross became heaven's family tree. Paradise was restored.

Jerusalem, the Future Capital

Jerusalem will become the capital of the world during the one thousand year reign of Christ. During His rule, Jerusalem becomes the spiritual and political center of all activity. Christ is King of the world and David is prince over Jerusalem

Once a year during the Feast of Tabenacles, all nations must attend the Tabernacles celebration or suffer the consequences of no rain in their nation for the coming year. This feast, the seventh and final of Israel's yearly celebrations, has a final day called the water drawing ceremony. The ritual was designed to draw attention to the importance of rain for the coming year. Those in the future who refuse to honor this feast will receive no rain for their crops:

"And it shall come to pass that everyone who is left of all the nations

which came against Jerusalem shall go up from year to year to worship the King, the LORD of hosts, and to keep the Feast of Tabernacles. And it shall be that, whichever of the families of the earth do not come up to Jerusalem to worship the King, the LORD of hosts, on them there will be no rain. If the family of Egypt will not come up and enter in, they shall have no rain; they shall receive the plague with which the LORD strikes the nations who do not come up to keep the Feast of Tabernacles. This shall be the punishment of Egypt and the punishment of all the nations that do not come up to keep the Feast of Tabernacles." – ZECHARIAH 14:16-19

In that day Jerusalem will be expanded to cover hundreds of square miles. It will be divided up between the priests, the Levites, and the people. For one thousand years, the righteous will rule and reign with Christ from God's favorite place—Jerusalem.

Finally, Heaven on Earth

When a minister preaches that we will live in heaven forever, he is partially correct. A believer with a resurrected body will always have access to heaven, but in the future, heaven will literally come down to earth.

John describes this event in Revelation chapters 21 and 22. He saw past the one thousand year reign of Christ into the events that would follow the one thousand years. The first event was a judgment called the Great White Throne judgment. Following this heavenly tribunal, lost souls will be expelled to the lake of fire, marked as the second death.

Following the prophetic order, all saints at that time will be in heaven to view this final judgment. Afterwards, the earth and the heavens will be purged with fire. Fire not only consumes objects but serves as a cleansing agent to remove disease, germs, and so forth. As God re-creates the earth,

John noticed that there were no more seas. I believe the purging fire will evaporate the waters that separate the continents, and that the land will move back as one large plate, just as some scientists believe existed in ages past. It appears that the continents were once joined together and that, through some catastrophic event, they were separated into individual land masses, or continents. This division may have occurred at the time of the fall of Lucifer when the earth was without form and void (Genesis 1:2). Others suggest it happened in the time of Peleg. The Scripture reveals that "in his day, the earth was divided" (Genesis 10:25). More Biblical researchers identify the flood of Noah as the possible cause of the shifting of the continents.

The removal of the seas through evaporation will once again give an opportunity for the earth to be watered by the river of life that will proceed from the throne of God in the city New Jerusalem. This life-giving water has sustained the trees of life in the heavenly city since time immortal (Revelation 22:1). Just as the ancient earthly garden was watered by one main river that branched into four directions, the water of life will be the main water source in the New Jerusalem

This Holy City with twelve foundations is fifteen hundred miles wide and fifteen hundred miles high. The Lamb is in the midst (center) of the city. Thousands of years before, in the earthly Eden, God communed with Adam at the tree of life which was in the midst (center) of the garden. The new Eden will mirror the old Eden, in that there will be no sin, no pain, no sickness, and no death (Revelation 21:4). Satan and his hideous hordes of vicious demons will be expelled forever from the new earth and confined in the lake of fire for eternity (Revelation 20:10).

Once again, God will commune directly with man in a garden of perfection. Evidence indicates that God's fellowship with man began in Eden's garden, in the location of what is now Jerusalem, and all prophetic events will conclude in Jerusalem. I have often said that Jerusalem was the road to heaven. The mystical symbolism, the spiritual significance, the Temple, the priesthood, and the sacrifices were all instituted in the city where God would "put His name."

If you wish to walk the path to heaven, you must pass through Jerusalem, to the hill of a skull, and bow and receive the sacrificial offering to redeem you from your sins. The road through Jerusalem will eventually lead to eternity, when the eternal Mount Zion and the heavenly city will shine with the light of the Lamb forever.

I believe Jerusalem is linked to the first Adam in the same manner as it is linked to the second Adam, Jesus Christ (1 Corinthians 15:45). God is worshipped in the mountain in heaven, just as He was worshipped on the Mountain of God on earth. Christ restored our access to the spiritual Temple in heaven and will, in the future, build an earthly Tabernacle in Jerusalem, where all men will come yearly to worship the King.

If you have never walked the path of Jerusalem, past the Temple to the cross of Christ where you will receive eternal life, may this book inspire you to receive forgiveness for your sins and begin a journey whose road through Jerusalem will lead you to the heavenly city.

Additional Notes and Points of Interest

1. Adam in Islamic Tradition

While discussing the concept of Israel being the center of the Garden of Eden, I was surprised when a Muslim friend, Joseph, began to share with me the Islamic tradition that the land of Palestine (Israel) was the area where Adam lived. He said that the area of the wilderness of Judea, near Jericho and the city of Adam, was where Adam lived after he was removed from the garden. We did not have time to document his source while preparing this manuscript, but he was very adamant that he was raised to understand this.

2. Jesus the Last Adam

Paul stated that Christ was the "last Adam:"

"And so it is written, the first man Adam was made a living soul; the last Adam was made a quickening spirit." – I CORINTHIANS 15:45

If the Adam of early creation was the first Adam, then Christ became the second Adam, or the last Adam. The parallels between the first Adam and the last Adam are interesting:

- The first Adam was created without a natural birth process of the seed of a man and a woman. He was formed by God from the dust. Jesus was born through a virgin but was conceived without the natural seed of a man, the seed being the Word of God!

- The first Adam had personal fellowship with God in a garden, and Christ had intimate communion with God in a garden (John 18:1-2).

- The first Adam encountered the serpent in the garden, while Christ had to encounter Satan throughout his ministry and, finally, in the Garden of Gethsemane (John 14:30).

- The first Adam lost his fellowship with God in the garden, but Christ submitted to the Father while interceding in the garden of Gethsemane (Matthew 26:36-39).

- When Adam fell, the ground was cursed and God said that he would sweat from his brow and deal with thorns (Genesis 3:18-19). Christ entered Gethsemane and as He prayed, His sweat became as it were great drops of blood (Luke 22:44). Later the soldiers placed a crown of thorns on His head, on the very area where His sweat became blood, indicating the parallel of Christ bearing the curse that was upon Adam and mankind (John 19:1-2).

- There were two trees in the Garden of Eden. One was the tree of life and the other the tree of knowledge of good and evil. God met Adam during the cool of the day at the tree of life (Genesis 3:8). The serpent, however, was at the tree of knowledge of good and evil which was located in the same area as the tree of life (Genesis 3:1-6). If the tree of life was planted on the future Temple Mount and the tree of knowledge was on the Mount of Olives near Bethphage (Matthew 21:1), and if Christ hung from the tree from the top of the Mount of Olives as some suggest, then He was crucified facing the previous location of the tree of life with His back to the area of the tree of knowledge of good and evil. His cursing of the fig tree indicated that a curse was now being placed in the area where the curse originated and where Adam and Eve sewed the fig leaves together!

- Just as God put Adam to sleep to remove a rib and create his wife Eve (Genesis 2:22), after Christ died (fell asleep), the centurion pierced Christ's side with a spear and blood and water poured out (John 19:34). From Christ's side would come forth a new bride: the church (2 Corinthians 11:2; Revelation 19:7-8). After Adam's fall it took a blood covering (death of two animals) to cover their transgression from God (Genesis 3:21). It would take the sacrifice of Christ to atone for the sins of all mankind (Romans 5:17-19).

- When Adam was expelled from the Garden, he traveled east, which would have lead him to the area of the Dead Sea, near what is today Jericho. Above Jericho, near the waters of the Jordan River, is the City of Adam. When Christ began His ministry, two major events occurred near Jericho. Christ was baptized in the Jordan River near the area of Jericho, where Joshua had once crossed with the children of Israel and where John baptized people in the wilderness (Joshua 3:16; 4:19-21;

John 3:22-23). Christ immediately went into the mountains of Judea where He was tempted of the devil. This area, according to tradition, is above Jericho where the spies hid after leaving Rahab's house in Jericho (Joshua 2:22).

The baptismal site and the location of the temptation in the wilderness (Matthew 4:1), was within the rage of 10 to 15 miles from the ancient city of Adam, where the water from the Jordan once stood as a heap when Joshua and Israel crossed from the wilderness into the Promised Land. Why would God lead Christ into the wilderness to the same area where the first Adam may have ventured after the fall? To complete the patterns of redemption! Christ went into the very wilderness where Adam had to sweat and labor because of the curse, and He faced the same devil (Satan) who had caused the fall of Adam over 4,000 years before!

- The first Adam was tempted with:

    1. Lust of the flesh: the fruit was good for food (Genesis 3:6)

    2. Lust of the eyes: the fruit was pleasant to the eyes (Genesis 3:6)

    3. Pride of life : the fruit from the tree will make you wise (Genesis 3:6)

- Christ, the last Adam, was tempted with:

    1. Lust of the flesh: turn the stones to bread (Matthew 4:3)

    2. Lust of the eyes: throw yourself down from this high spot (Matthew 4:6)

> 3. Pride of life: I will give you the kingdoms of the world (Matthew 4:9)

The last Adam overcame the temptations of Satan in the wilderness to demonstrate that He had spiritual authority over the devil. The location of both activities was about 18 miles from the area of the city of Adam.

There are many parallels between the first and last Adam. Since Christ's life and ministry would bring victory in every area where the first Adam sinned, then God allowed Christ to come to the same geographical location where Adam lost his spiritual heritage so that Christ could restore lost paradise back to man; thus the need to return to Jerusalem.

3. The Two Altars in Jerusalem

In their book, *The Rod and the Almond Tree,* Dr. Peter Michas and Robert Vander Maten make an interesting point about two different altars in Jerusalem.

According to Torah Anthology, Adam constructed the first altar on the Temple Mount. Generations later, the same altar was rebuilt by Abel, Noah, and Abraham. Dr. Michas points out that in such passages as Genesis 4:4, 8:20, and 22:9, the word built in Hebrew is *banah.* The word can also allude to rebuilding or restoring an altar. From this insight comes the idea that the same altar on the Temple Mount was revisited by the patriarchs and rebuilt over many generations.

However, there were two separate altars in Jerusalem. When the plague struck Jerusalem in David's time, David purchased the threshing floor of a Jebusite, rebuilt the altar, and offered a blood sacrifice to prevent the judgment angel from destroying Jerusalem. There are two separate Biblical references to David purchasing a threshing floor and building (rebuilding) an altar in Jerusalem. Without further research, these references could appear to indicate an error or contradiction.

The first reference is in 2 Samuel 24. David went to the threshing floor of **Ornan** the Jebusite and purchased the area with 600 shekels of gold (2 Samuel 24:21-26). This area, Mount Moriah, became the location where the Temple of Solomon would later be built (2 Chronicles 3:1). Another Biblical writer in Chronicles records that David purchased a threshing floor from **Araunah** the Jebusite for 50 shekels of silver. Scholars have observed that these two names are different (Ornan and Araunah) and that the cost differs—600 shekels in gold and 50 shekels in silver. Most people believe it is one single event told by two different writers. Some liberal scholars mark this as a contradiction in Scripture or an error created by a copyist. However, there may be another reason for the two names and two different costs.

There were two altars established in Jerusalem: a brass altar at the Temple and a stone altar on the Mount of Olives. A special sacrifice occurred on the Mount of Olives, and it involved a red heifer (see Numbers 19). This red female cow was burnt "without (outside) the gate" which, after Israel possessed the land, was on the Mount of Olives facing the Temple Mount. This was not the same altar made of brass from which the daily sacrifices at the Temple were performed. The brazen altar was located near the doors of the Temple. The red heifer altar was situated halfway up the Mount of Olives, which would have been about 2,000 cubits or 3,000 feet away from the brass altar at the Temple.

It is possible that David purchased two altars. The threshing floor of Ornan was located on Mount Moriah, and it was a larger area that would have been worth much more money (600 gold shekels). Since the angel of destruction was on top of the Mount of Olives overlooking the east of Jerusalem (1 Chronicles 21:15-16), David also would have purchased the special altar (upon which the red heifer was offered), thus preventing the death angel from passing over from the Garden of Gethsemane into Jerusalem.

Gold was used to purchase the Temple Mount because gold represents deity and the Temple was God's House. The second altar on the Mount of Olives was purchased with silver which represents redemption. The site of the red heifer sacrifice would have been, according to some, the same general area where the future crucifixion tree (the cross) would be raised. Christ would one day face the Temple from the Mount of Olives, look over the wall into the open doors of the Holy Place, and see the cherubim on the curtain. The number fifty (50 shekels) is also the number of redemption and is linked to the year of Jubilee (Leviticus 25). If Christ was crucified in the area of the Mount of Olives altar (where the red heifer was offered), it fits a beautiful pattern of the last Adam restoring redemption to mankind, in the very area where Adam and Eve sinned and lost their eternal status.

The red heifer sacrifice was a perfect picture of Christ's sufferings and man's redemption. Just as the red heifer was offered outside the camp (the East Gate), Christ was crucified outside the camp (Hebrews 13:11-12), or outside the Eastern Gate in Jerusalem. Cedar wood, hyssop and scarlet were thrown in the midst of the burning heifer (Numbers 19:6). Christ was crucified on a wooden cross, a scarlet robe was placed on His back, and a soldier placed hyssop to His mouth (Matthew 27:28 and 32; John 19:29). The priest would observe the burning of the heifer while others performed the sacrifice, just as the priest looked on while the Romans placed Christ on the cross (John 19:6). The ashes of the red heifer were used as a water of purification to cleanse from uncleanness (Numbers 19:9). Christ's sacrifice of His blood was the final offering for sin (Hebrews 10:10).

David could have purchased both the threshing floor on Mount Moriah and the threshing floor on the Mount of Olives, two locations and two altars, as a preview of the future redemption of humanity! These two altars were located in the area of the two trees in the garden—one of life and one of knowledge of good and evil.

4. Back to the Garden of Eden

Why would the purchase of two altars be significant to the patterns of ancient Eden? If the tree of life was once on the same spot as the Temple Holy of Holies, and the tree of knowledge was once on the edge of the Mount of Olives, then the Temple altar was a picture of meeting with God, while the altar on the Mount of Olives was a picture of final redemption. If Christ was crucified on the Mount of Olives, then He fulfilled the offering of the red heifer at His crucifixion!

I believe there is ample evidence to prove that the area of Jerusalem is the center of the ancient Garden of Eden. This explains why Shem went to Salem (Jerusalem), why Abraham went to Mount Moriah, why David bought the two altars, why Solomon built the Temple there, and why Christ eventually ministered, was crucified, buried, and raised from the grave in the Holy City. It explains why Jerusalem is the apple of God's eye (Zechariah 2:2-8).

In the future, the resurrected saints will live, rule, and reign in the very place that was marked by the Almighty from the days that He formed man from the dust of Eden!

Bibliography

Adam Clark Commentary, PC Study Bible Software

Barnes Notes, PC Study Bible Software

Dakes Annotated Bible, published by Dakes Bible Sales, P. O. Box 1050, Lawrenceville, GA 30246

Garrard, Alec. *The Splendor of the Temple,* Grand Rapids, MI: Kregel Publications, 2000

Jamieson, Fausset, and Brown Commentaries, PC Study Bible Software

Martin, Ernest L. *Secrets of Golgotha,* Portland, OR: ASK Publications, 1988

Michas, Peter. *The Rod and the Almond Tree,* Mukiltoe, WA: Winepress Publishing, 1997

Nun, Mendal. *The Sea of Galilee and Its Fisherman in the New Testament,* Kibbutz Ein Gev, Israel: Kennereth Sailing Company, 1989

The Book of Jasher, Translated from the Hebrew, Muskogee, OK: Artisan Publishers, 1840 reprint

The Torah Anthology- Multi-Volume Set, Brooklyn, NY: Maznaim Publishing Corporation, 1977

Whiston, William (Translator). *Josephus, The Complete Works,* Grand Rapids, MI: Kregel Publications

Zlotowitz, Rabbi Meir (Translator). *ArtScroll Tanach Series: Genesis, Volume 1*

Updated Information on the Crucifixion of Jesus: www.asklem.com/doctrine

An illustration revealing the key locations written about in this book.

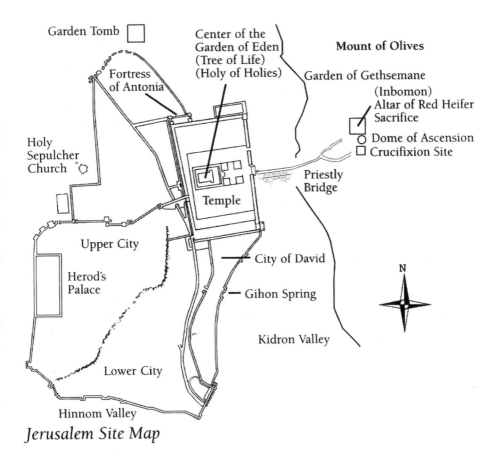

Garden Tomb

Center of the
Garden of Eden
(Tree of Life)
(Holy of Holies)

Mount of Olives

Fortress
of Antonia

Garden of Gethsemane
(Inbomon)
Altar of Red Heifer
Sacrifice

Holy
Sepulcher
Church

Dome of Ascension
Crucifixion Site

Temple

Priestly
Bridge

Upper City

City of David

Herod's
Palace

Gihon Spring

N

Kidron Valley

Lower City

Hinnom Valley

Jerusalem Site Map

This illustration is from the book *The Rod of an Almond Tree in God's Master Plan* by Peter A. Michas. Winepress Publishing

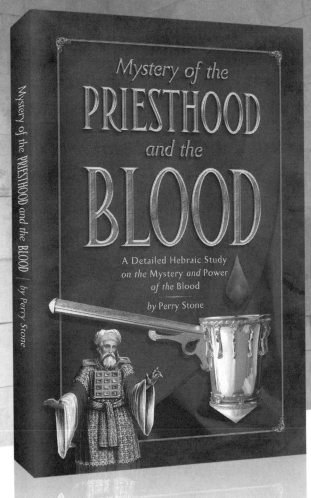

Two Powerful, Illustrated Messages

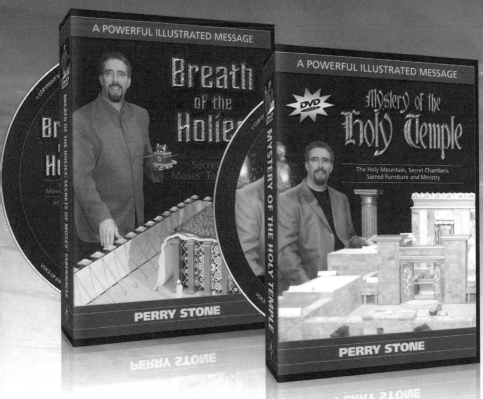

Breath of the Holies

This special 2-hour DVD is filled with incredible teaching on the secrets of Moses' Tabernacle. Learn the hidden meaning of the boards, fabrics, metals, and details of this mysterious tent. Learn of the geographical location of the heavenly temple, the throne room, sacred furniture, and worhip in the temple. This DVD also explores how Noah's Ark was a picture of the future tabernacle, how the cross is hidden in six places in the Old Testament and tabernacle, and how the secret place of the most high God is connected to the Ark of the Covenant and the wings of the cherub. If you love Hebraic teaching and learning fresh truths that will stir your spirit, this DVD is for you!

Item: DV086 (Breath of the Holies DVD)
Price: $20 Plus shipping & handling

Mystery of the Holy Temple

Mystery of the Holy Temple DVD is a special 2-hour teaching of Herod's temple. You will learn about the Mountains of God, hidden chambers under the Temple Mount in Jerusalem and the possible location of the lost Ark of the Covenant. Perry teaches with miniature models of the sacred furniture of the Temple and reveals hidden meaning, along with God's plan of redemption. Perry teaches of the six individuals who worked at the ancient temple, seven areas of the temple, as well as the worship, music and offerings at the temple. This Hebraic teaching will open your eyes to one of the great mysteries of God the sacred temple!

Item: DV085 (Mystery of the Holy Temple DVD)
Price: $20 Plus shipping & handling

For Credit Card orders call 423.478.3456
For additional resource materials please visit www.perrystone.org

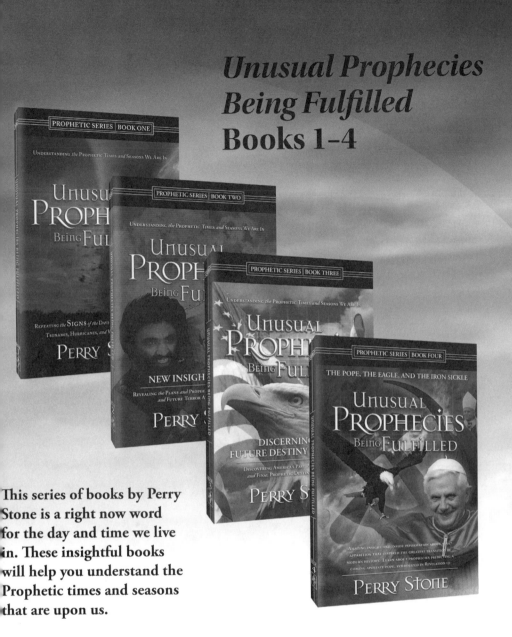